"It is good that a man should both hope and quietly wait for the salvation of the LORD."

I like to:
Seek quiet
Practice quiet
Grow in quiet
Study quiet
Take time to be quiet.

The way I use my prayer journal; I take a moment to sit quietly and think about all the wonderful and gracious things in your life.  It is so easy to keep track of the things that bring us heartache and worry.  But make a practice to take time each day to quiet your mind and heart…then when your mind is quiet, count those beautiful moments big and small.

When I first started practicing sitting quietly, my mind rebelled. It would start a litany of things I needed to do, things I wanted to do. Worries for others, or worries of my own. But with practice I learned to still those thoughts and look around me and truly enjoy the moment.

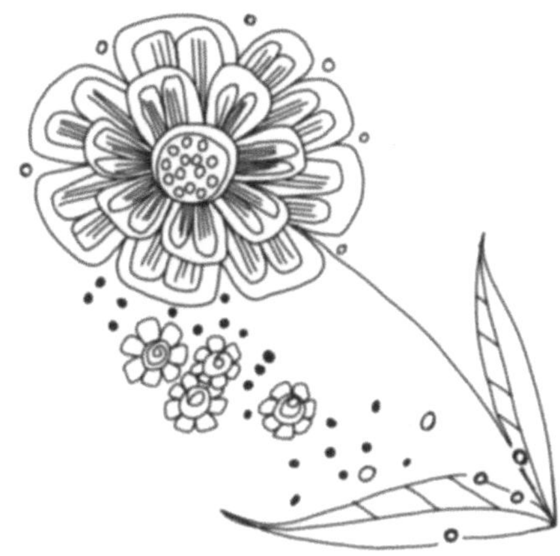

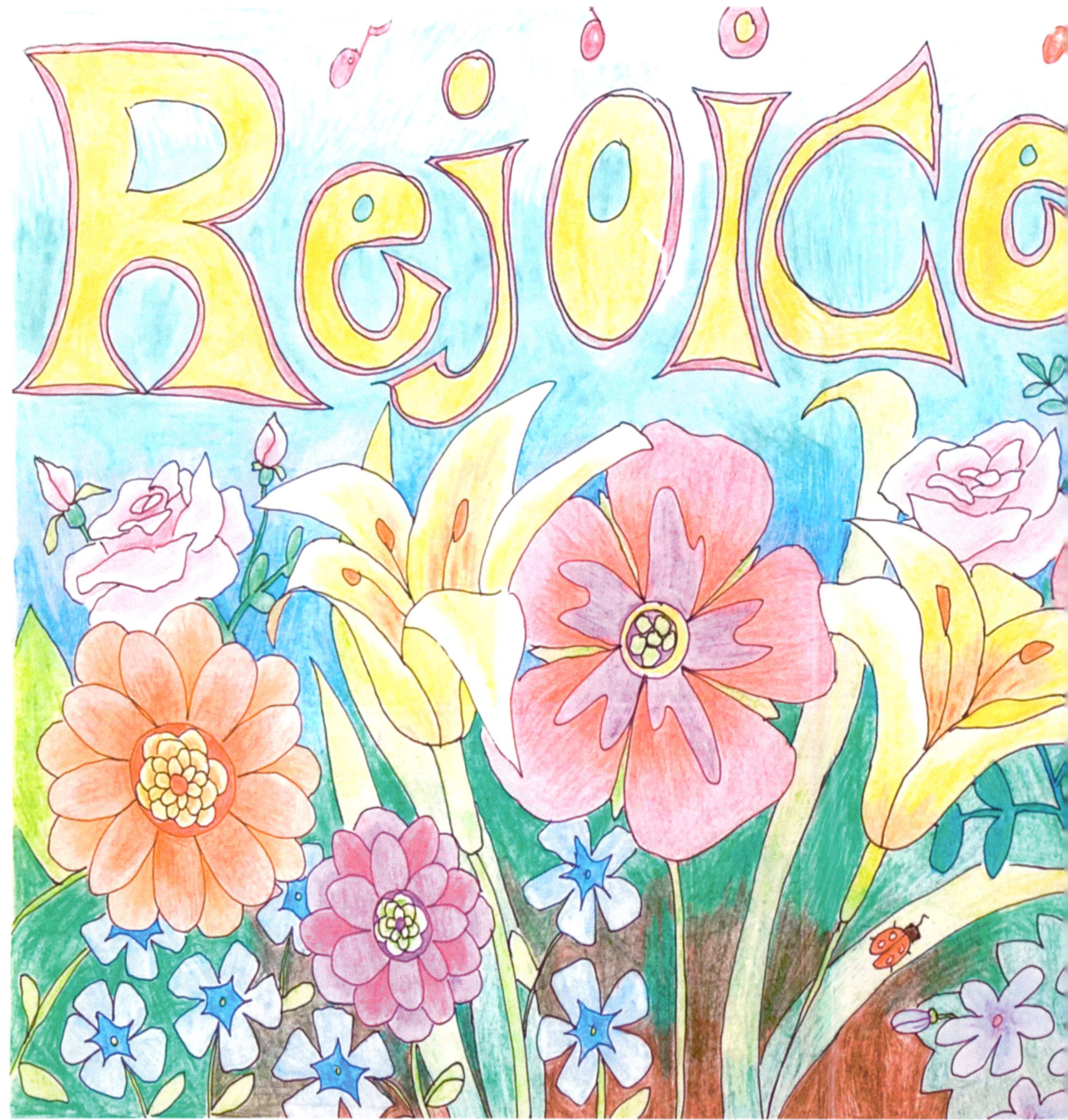

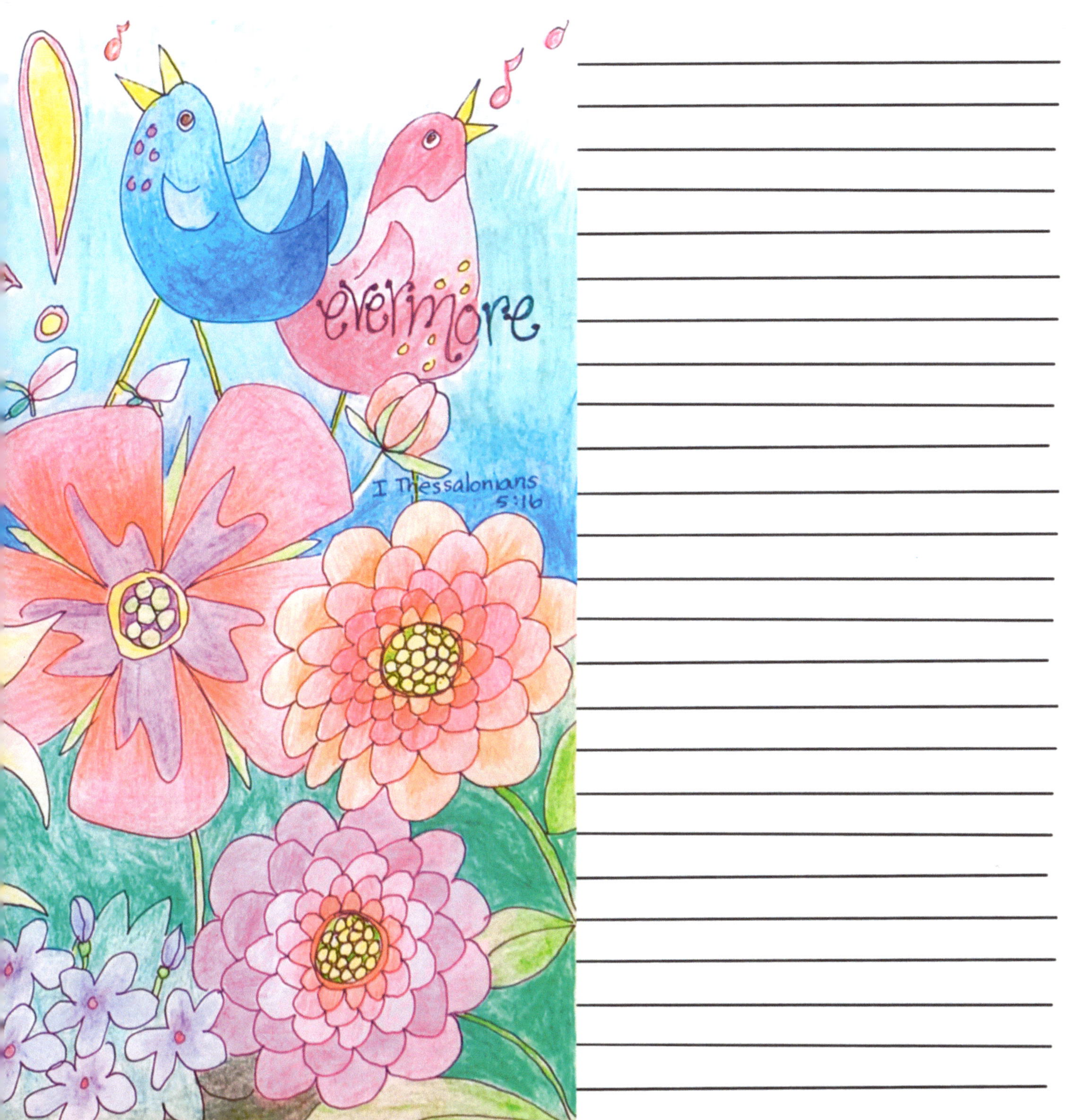

evermore
I Thessalonians 5:16

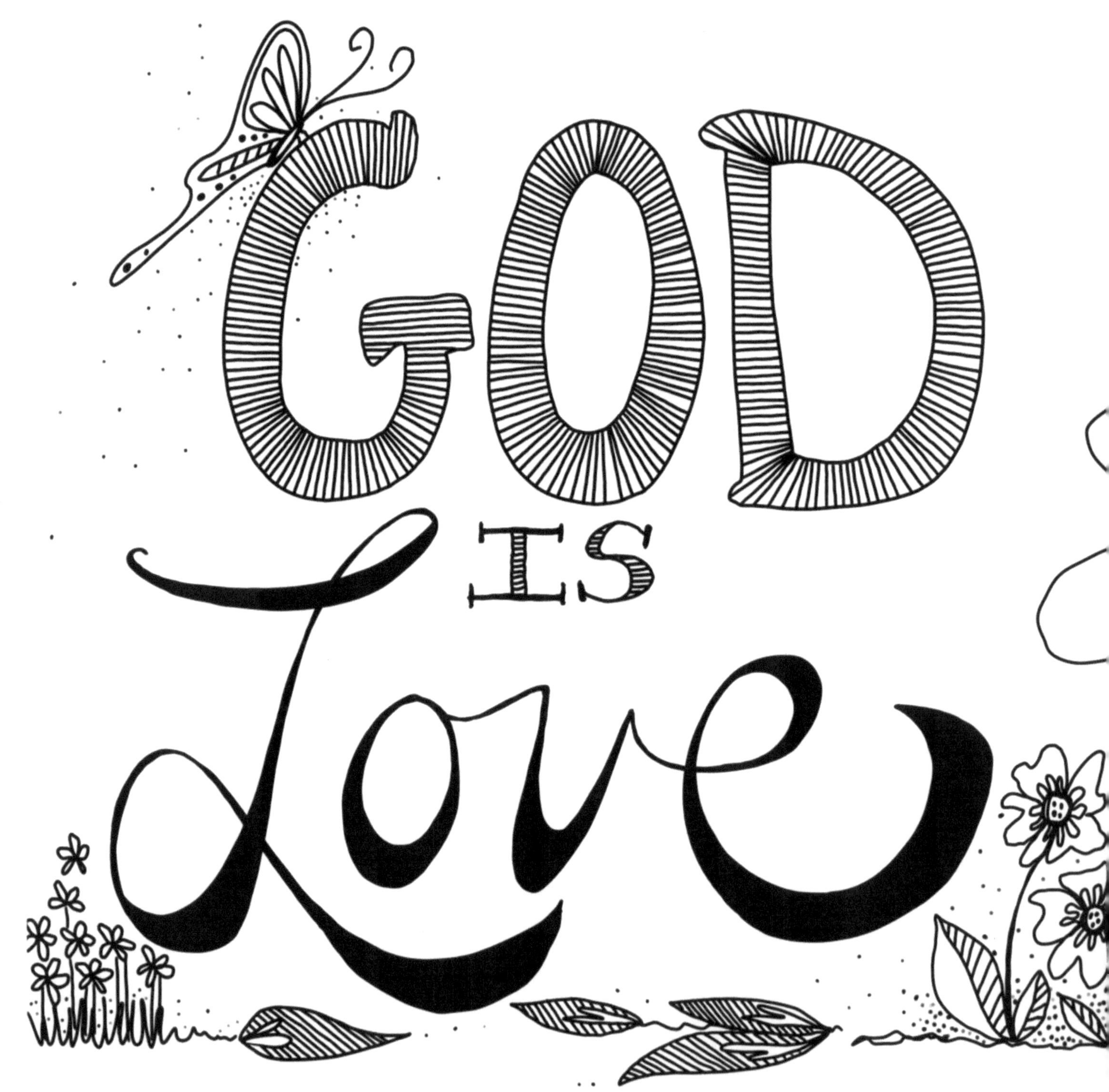

GOD
IS
Love

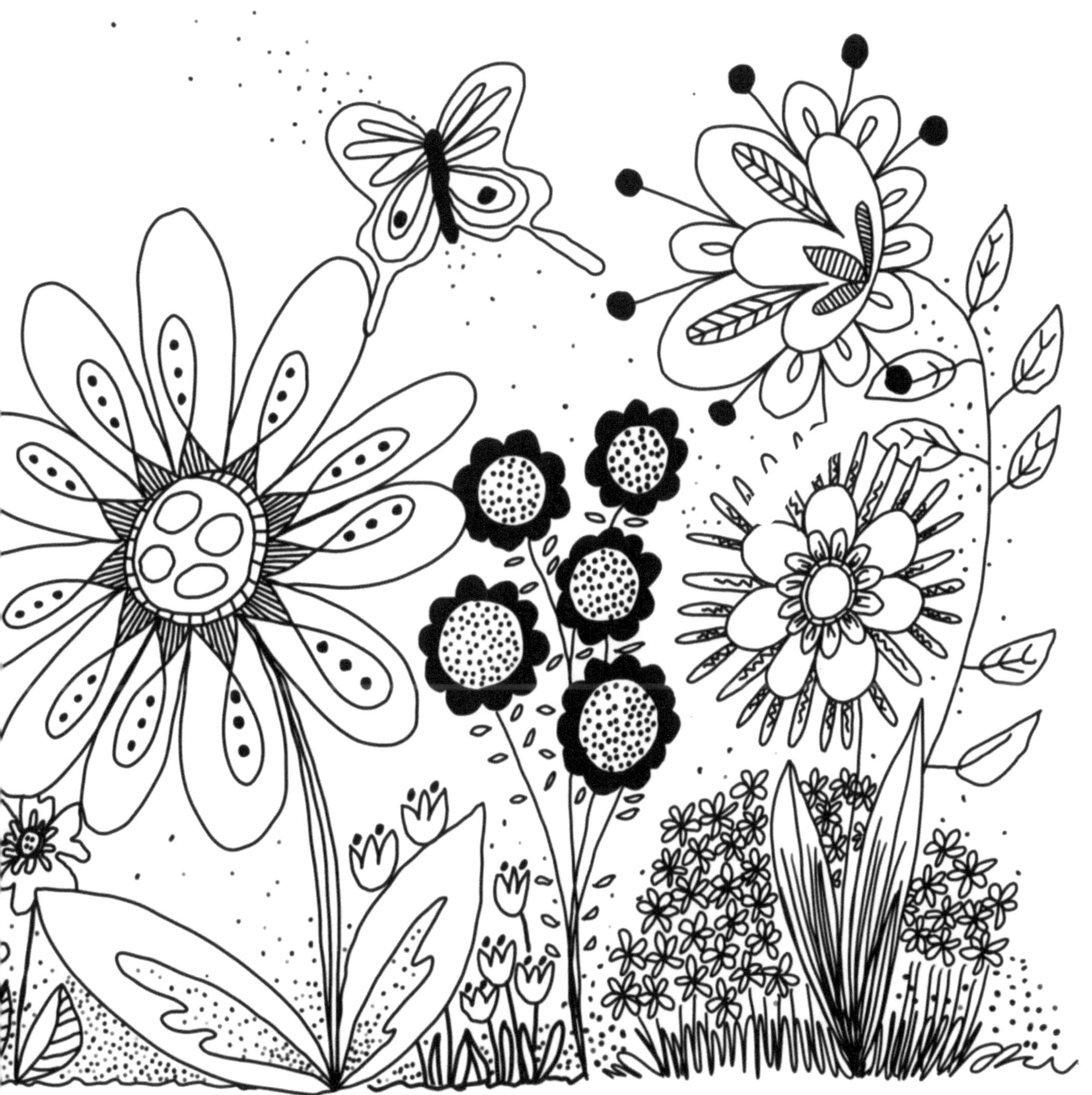

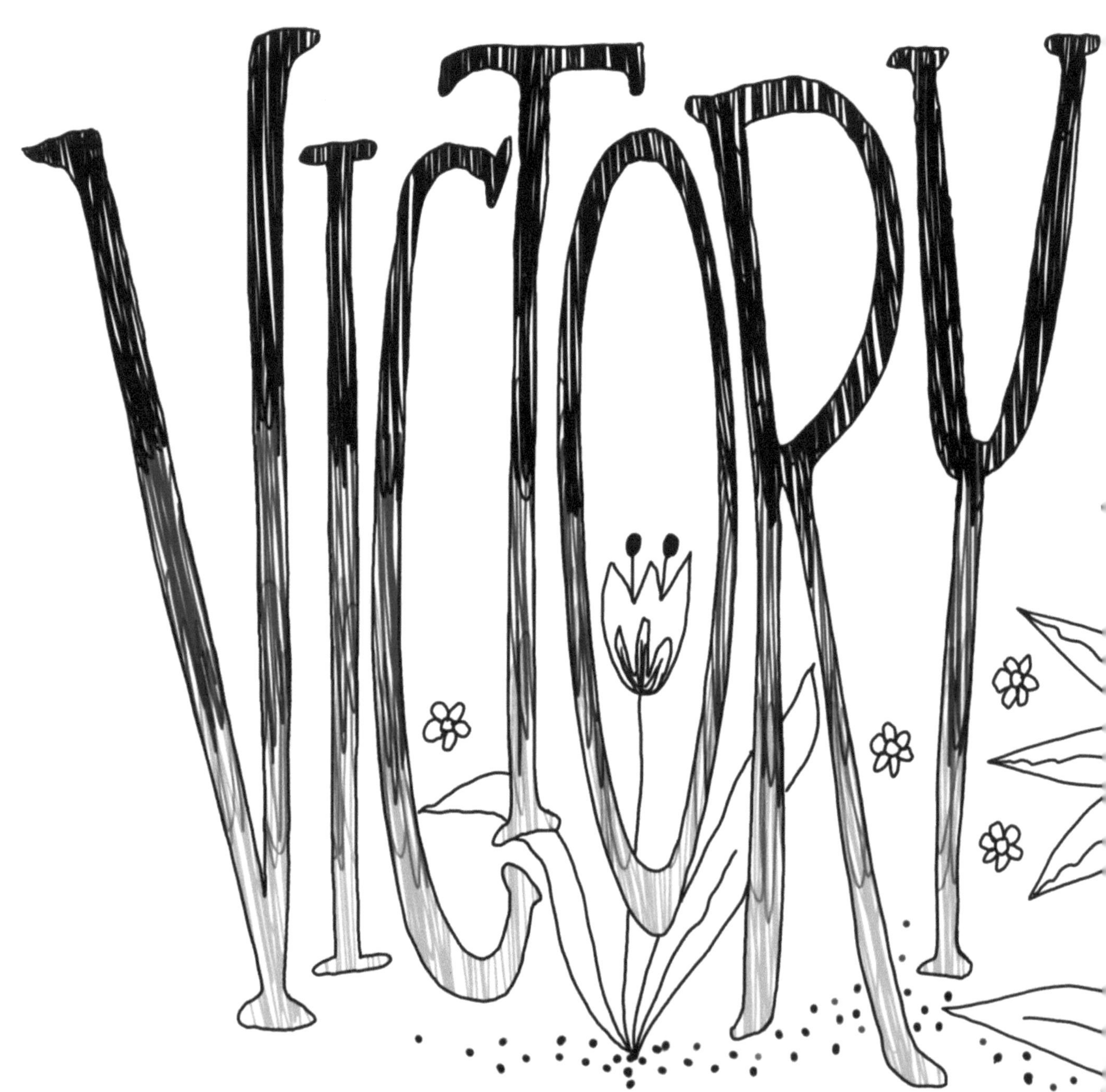
VICTORY

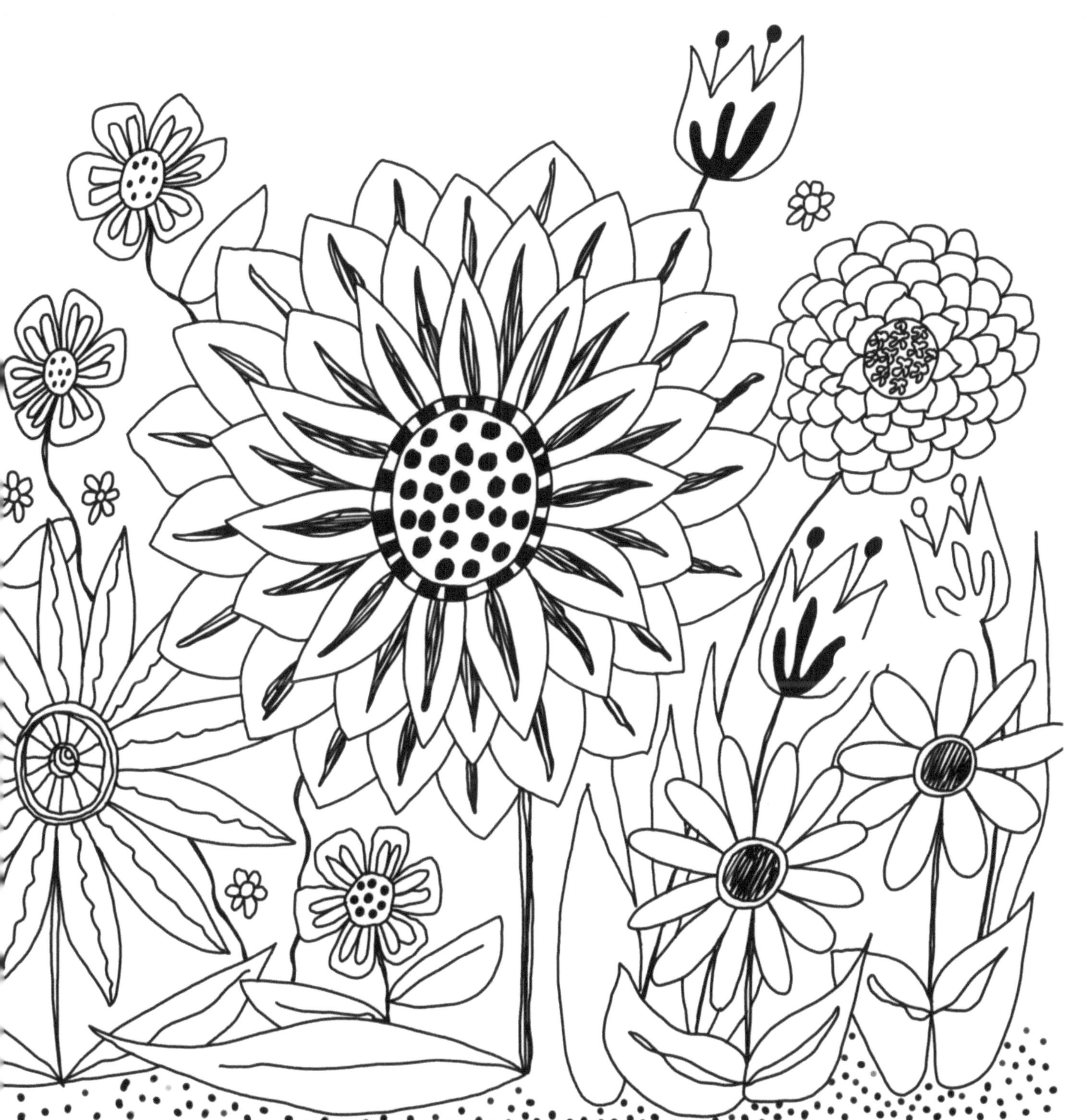

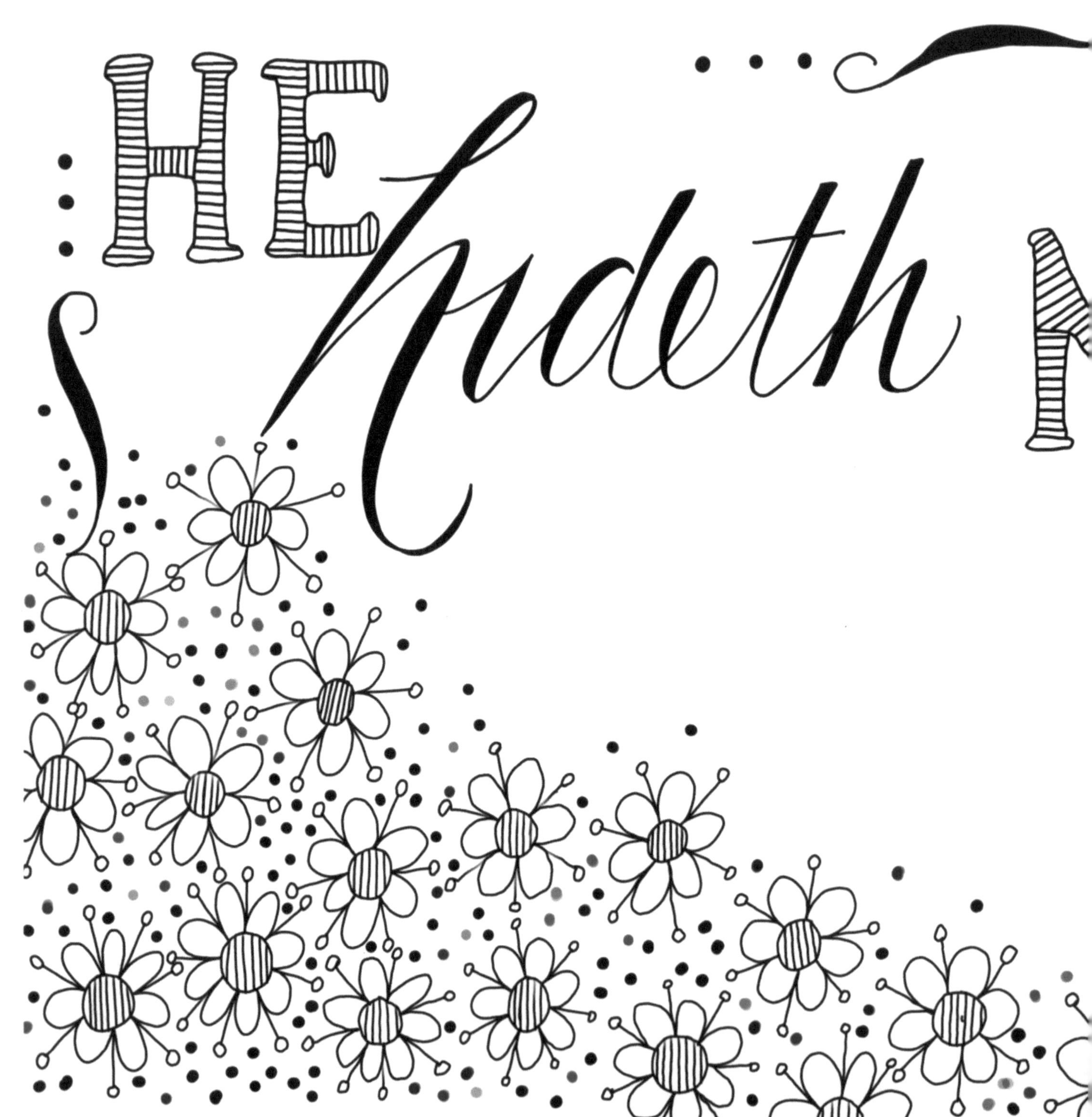
HE
hideth
M

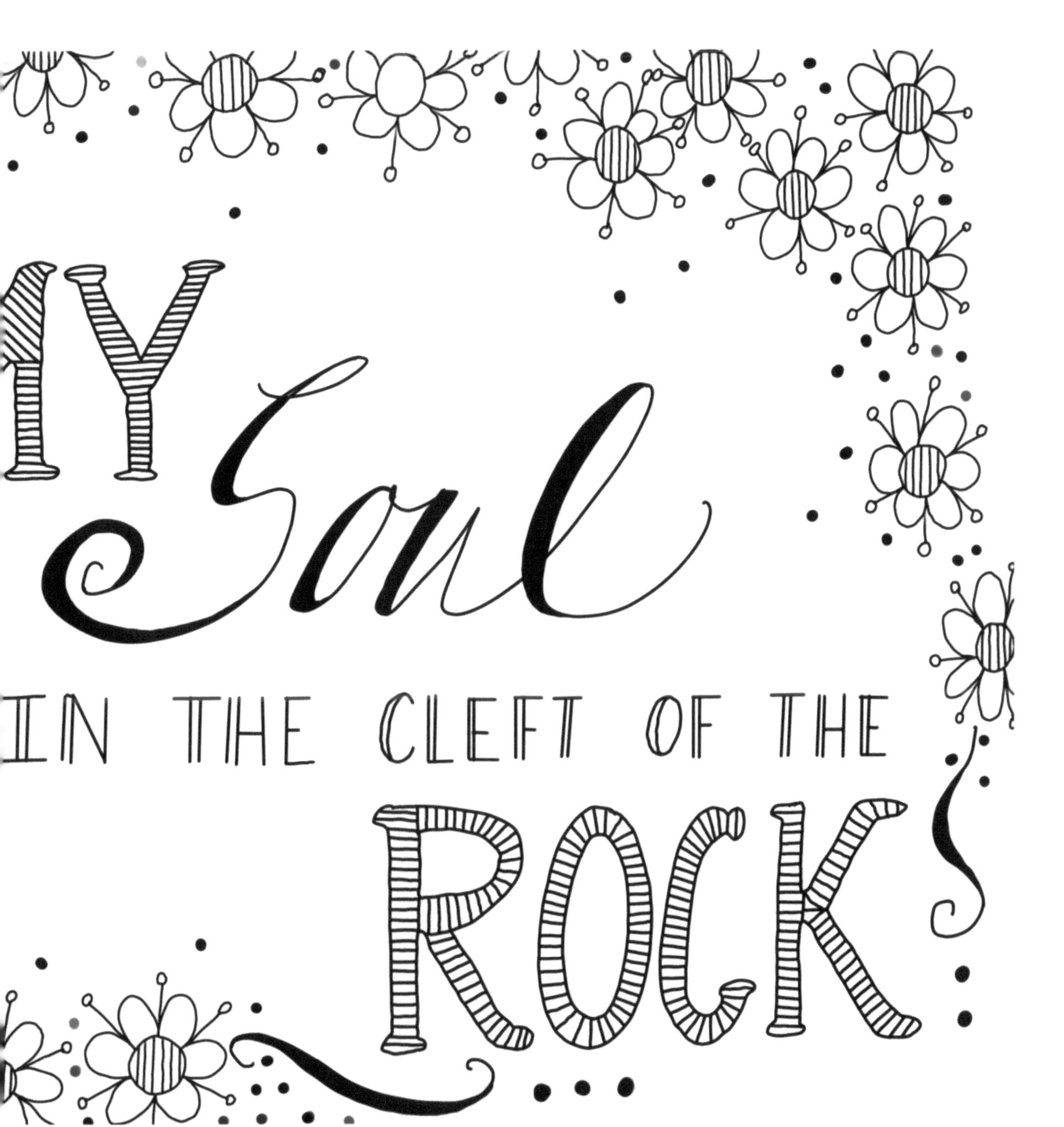

MY
Soul
IN THE CLEFT OF THE
ROCK

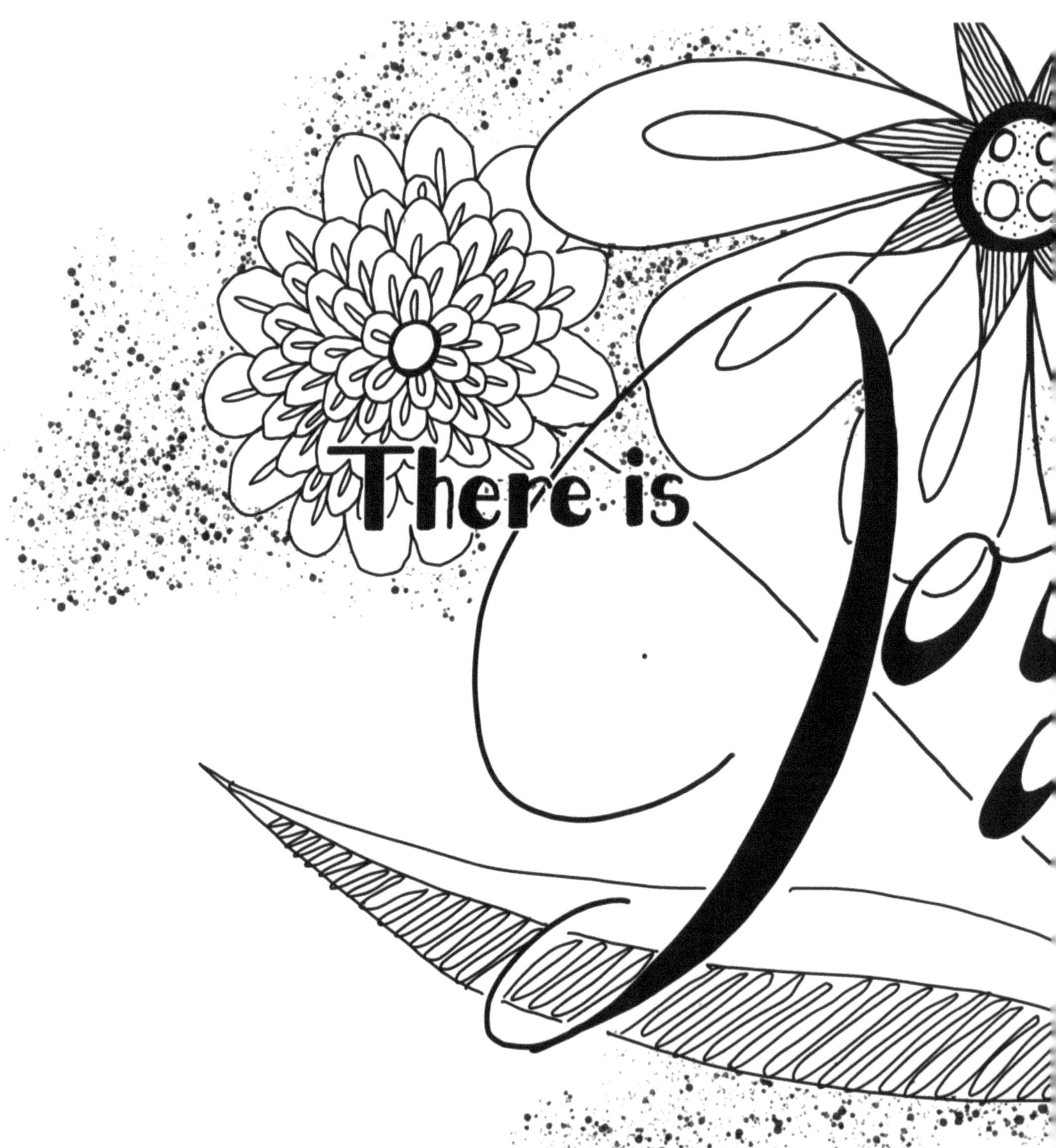
There is

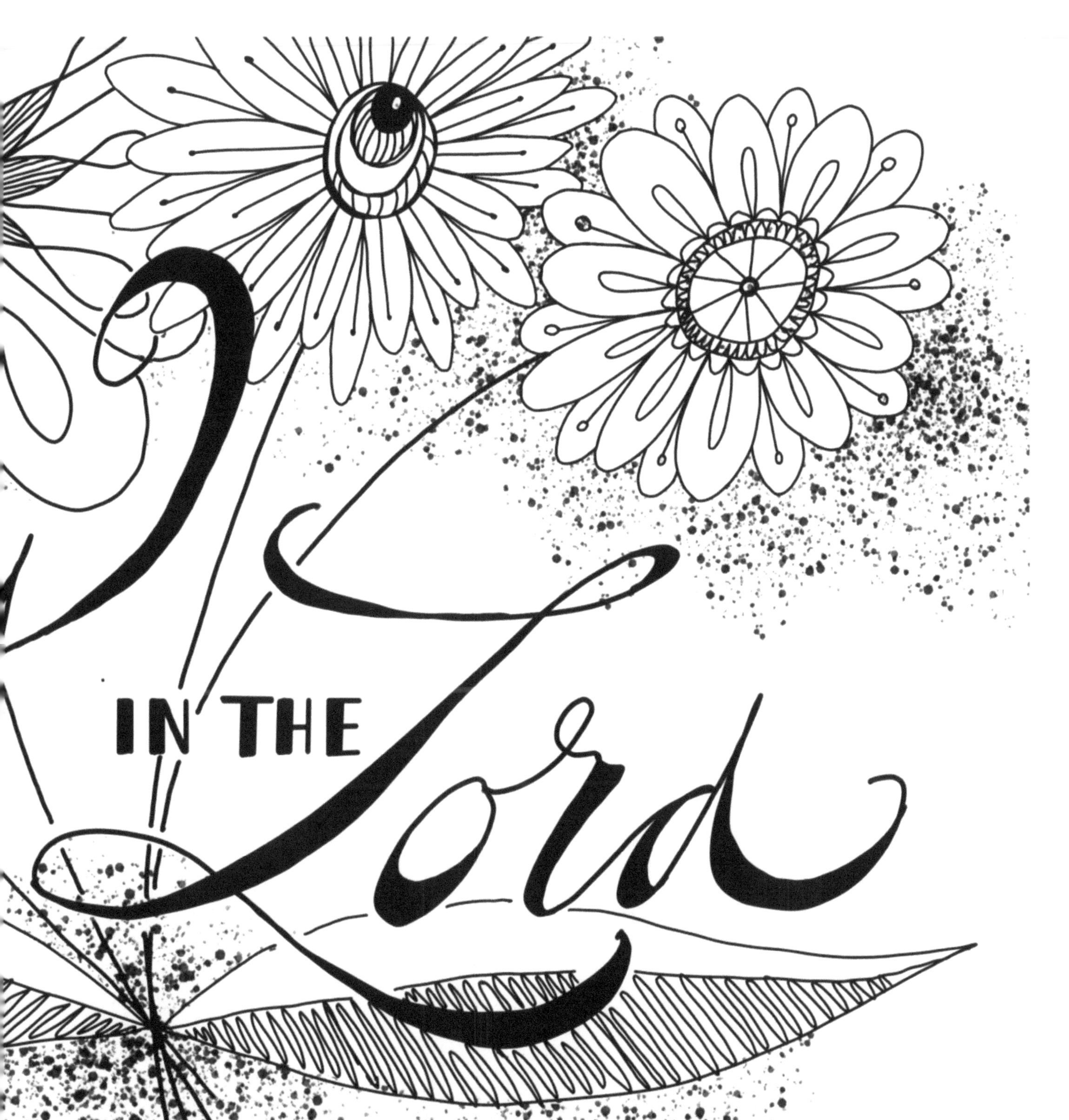

IN THE
Lord

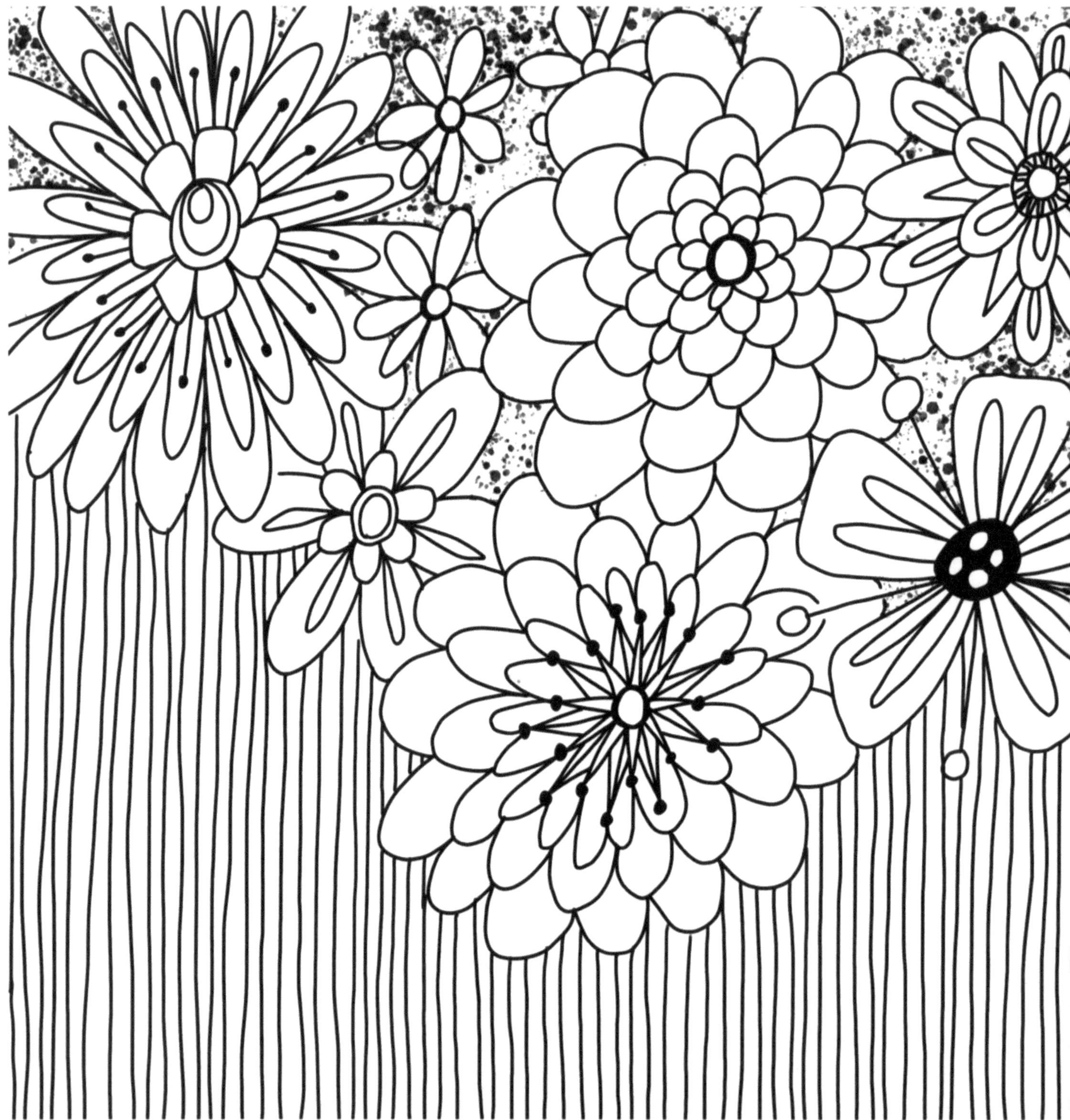

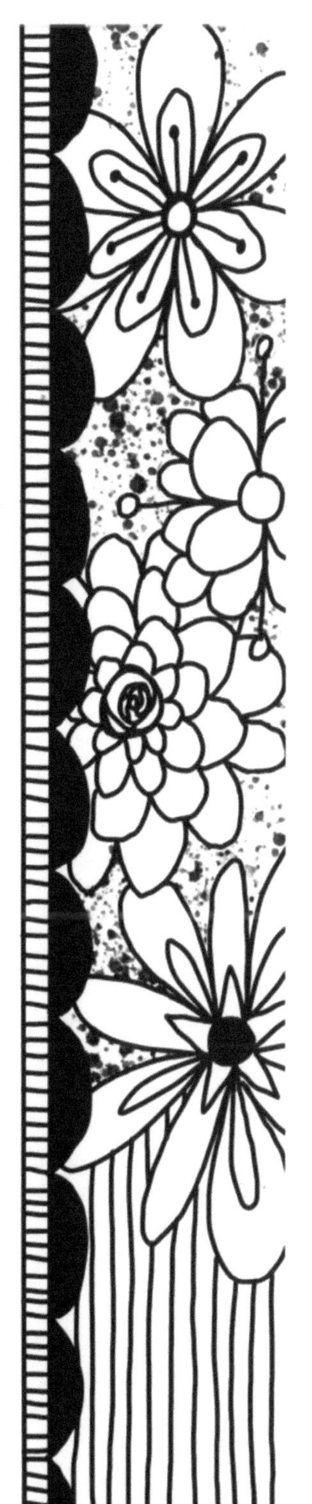

his
Hand
is
Guiding
me

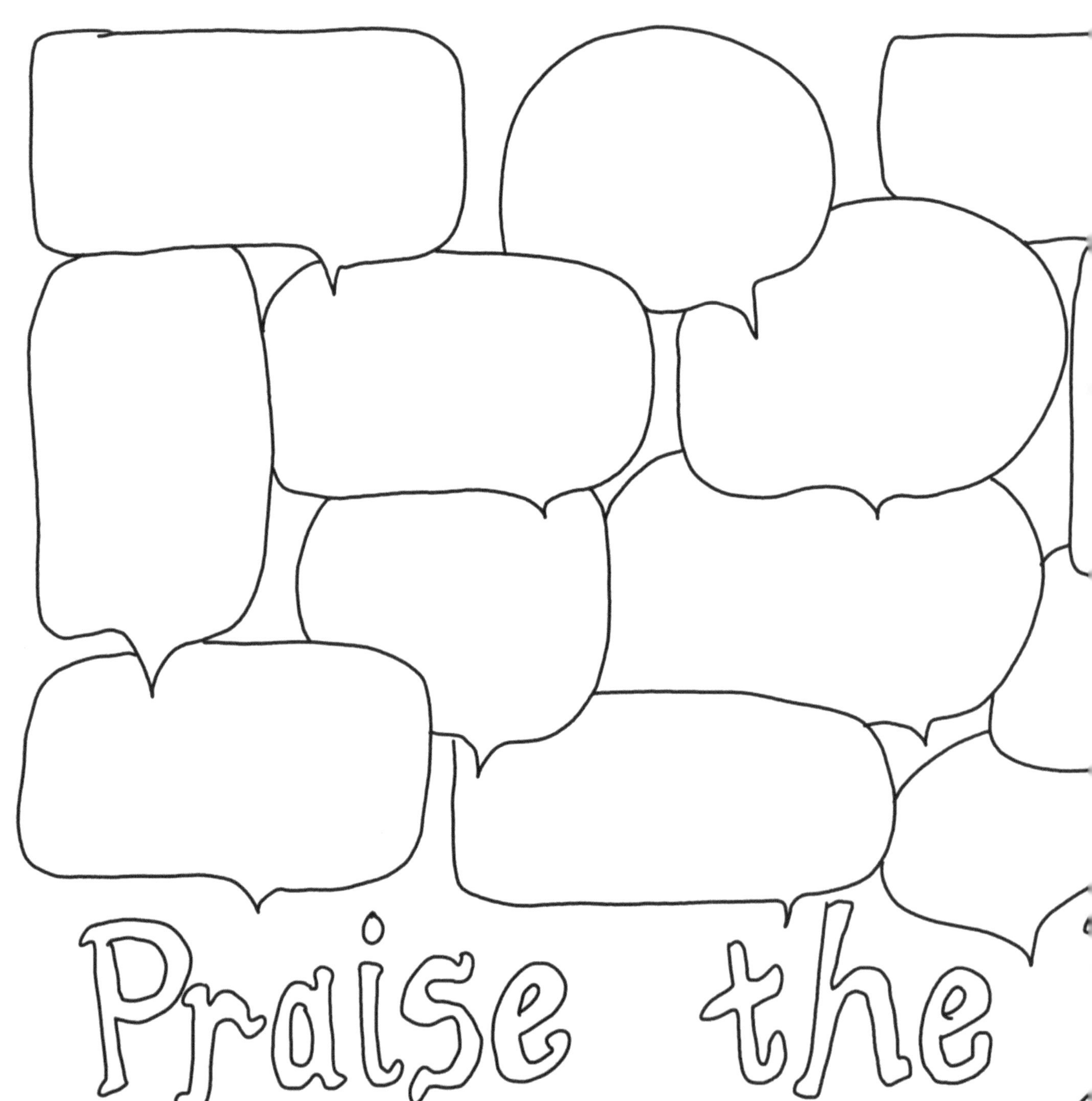

Praise the

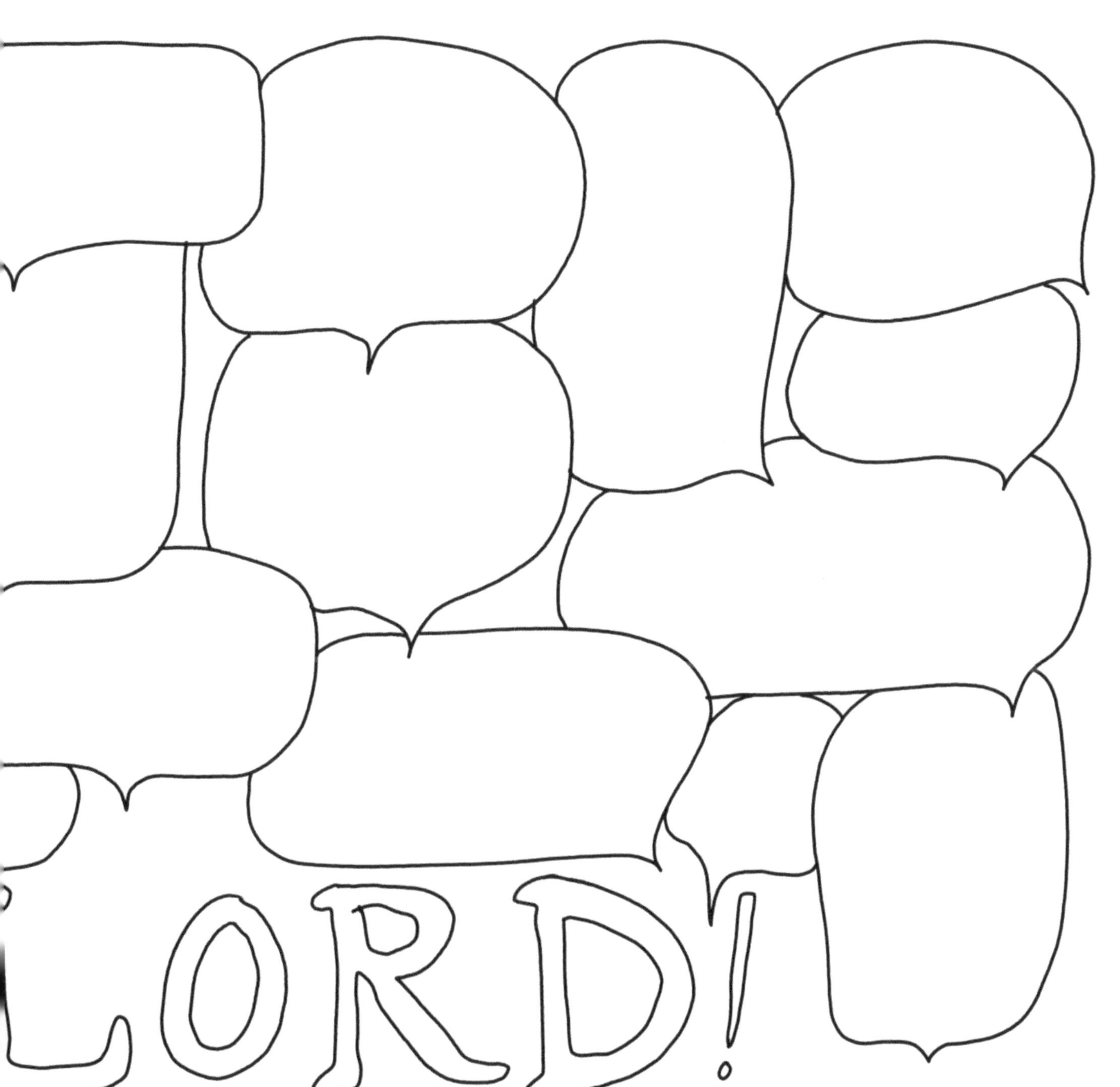

LORD!

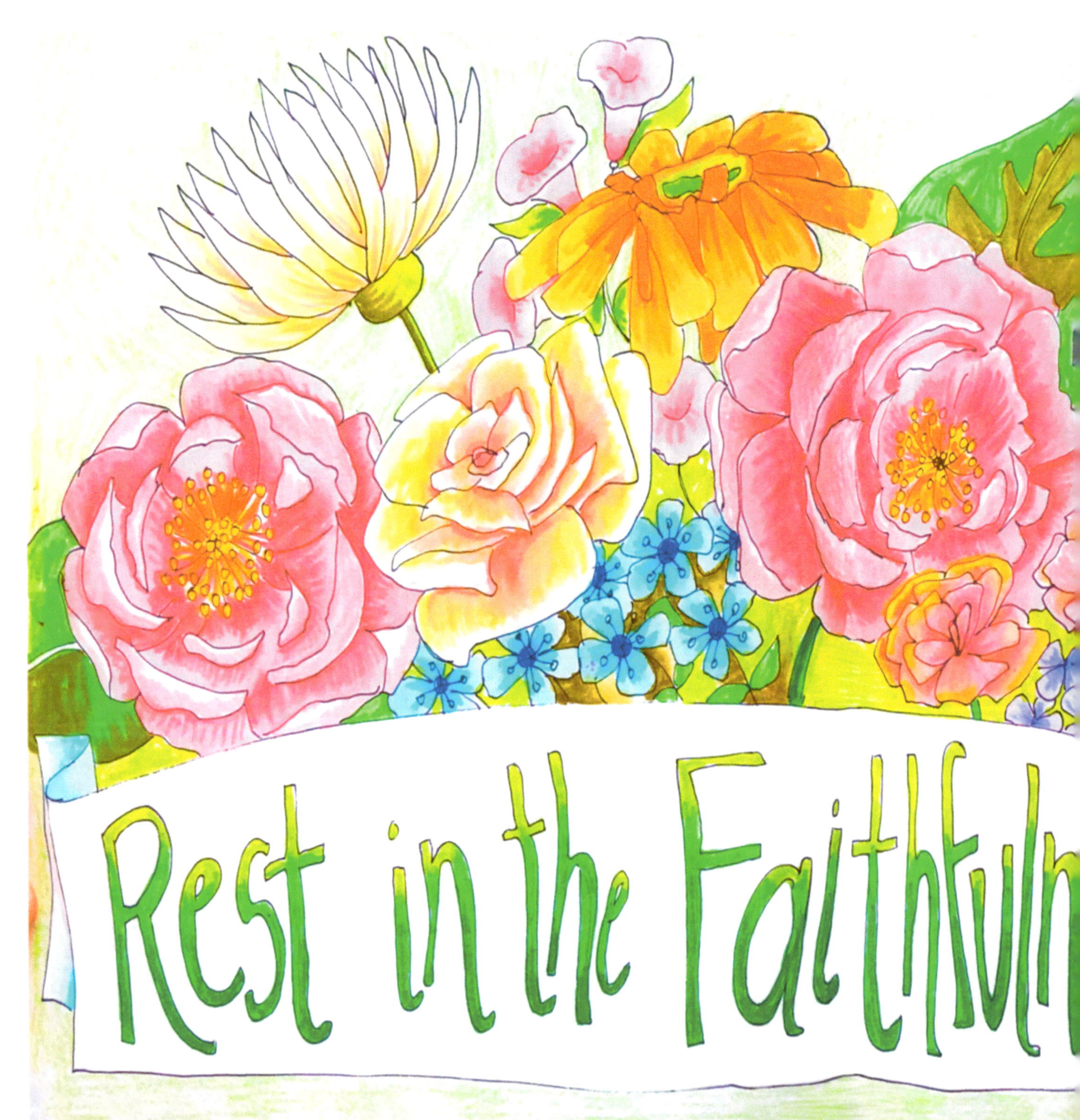

Rest in the Faithfuln

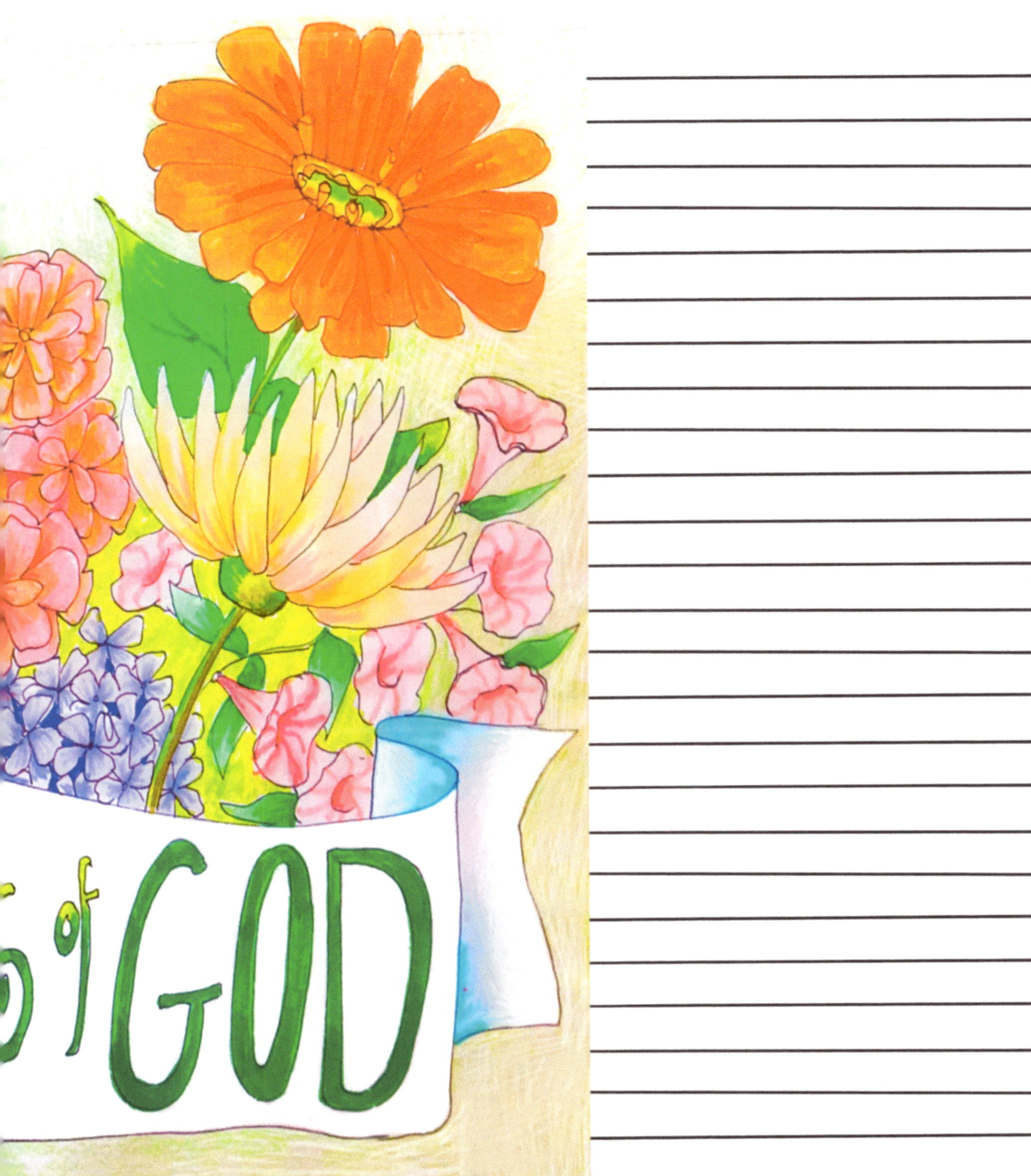
of GOD

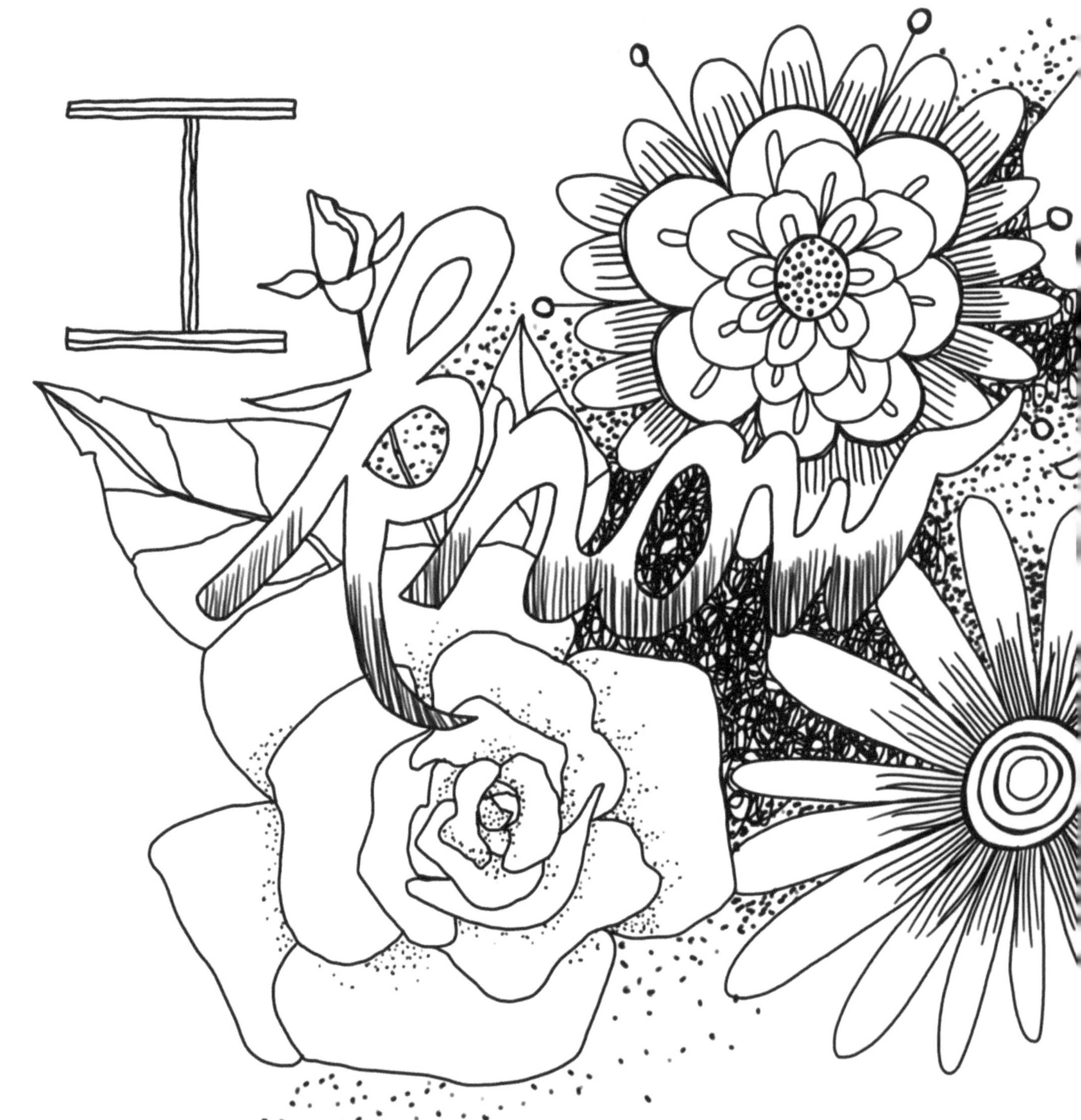

I Bloom

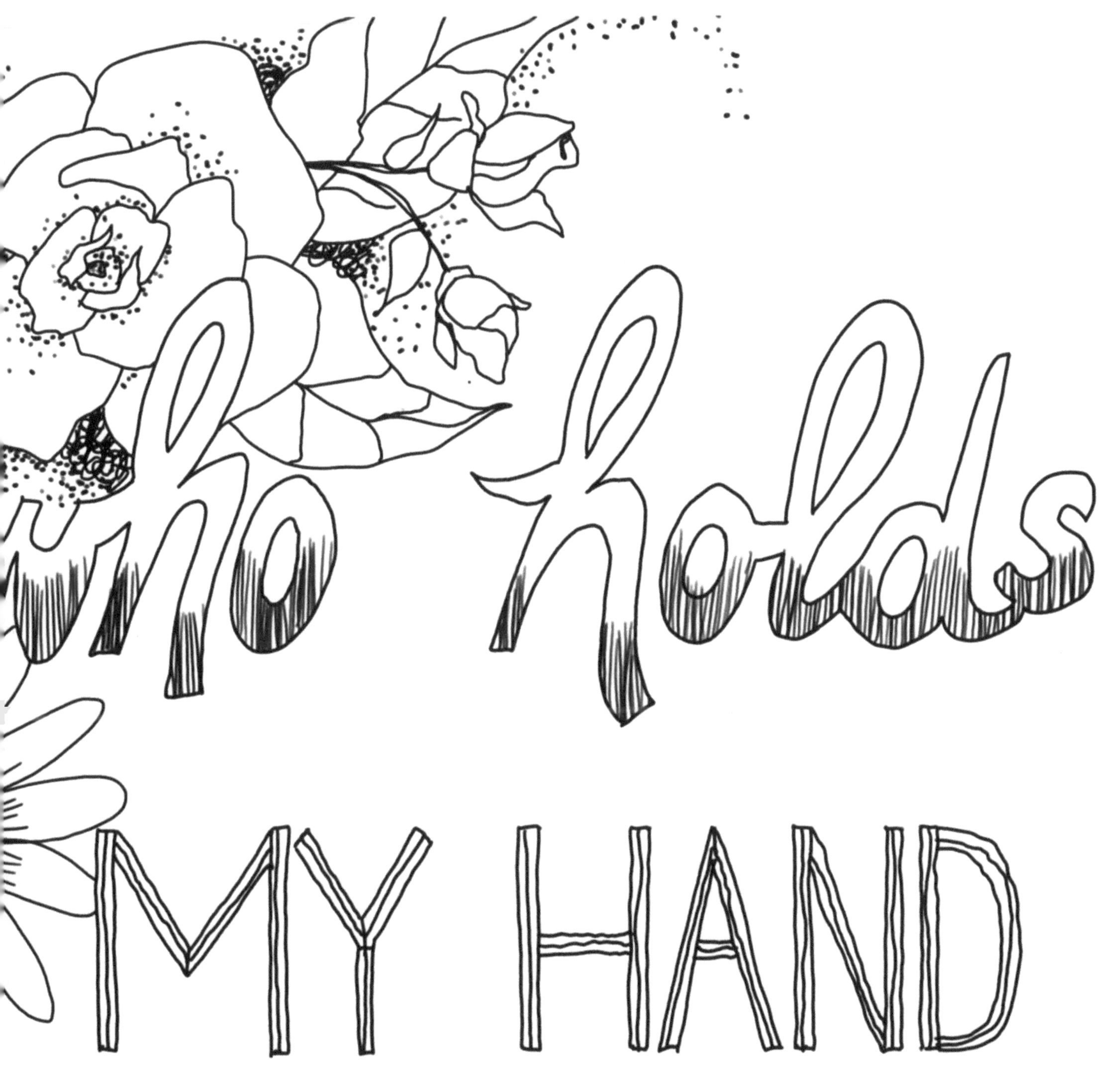

who holds
MY HAND

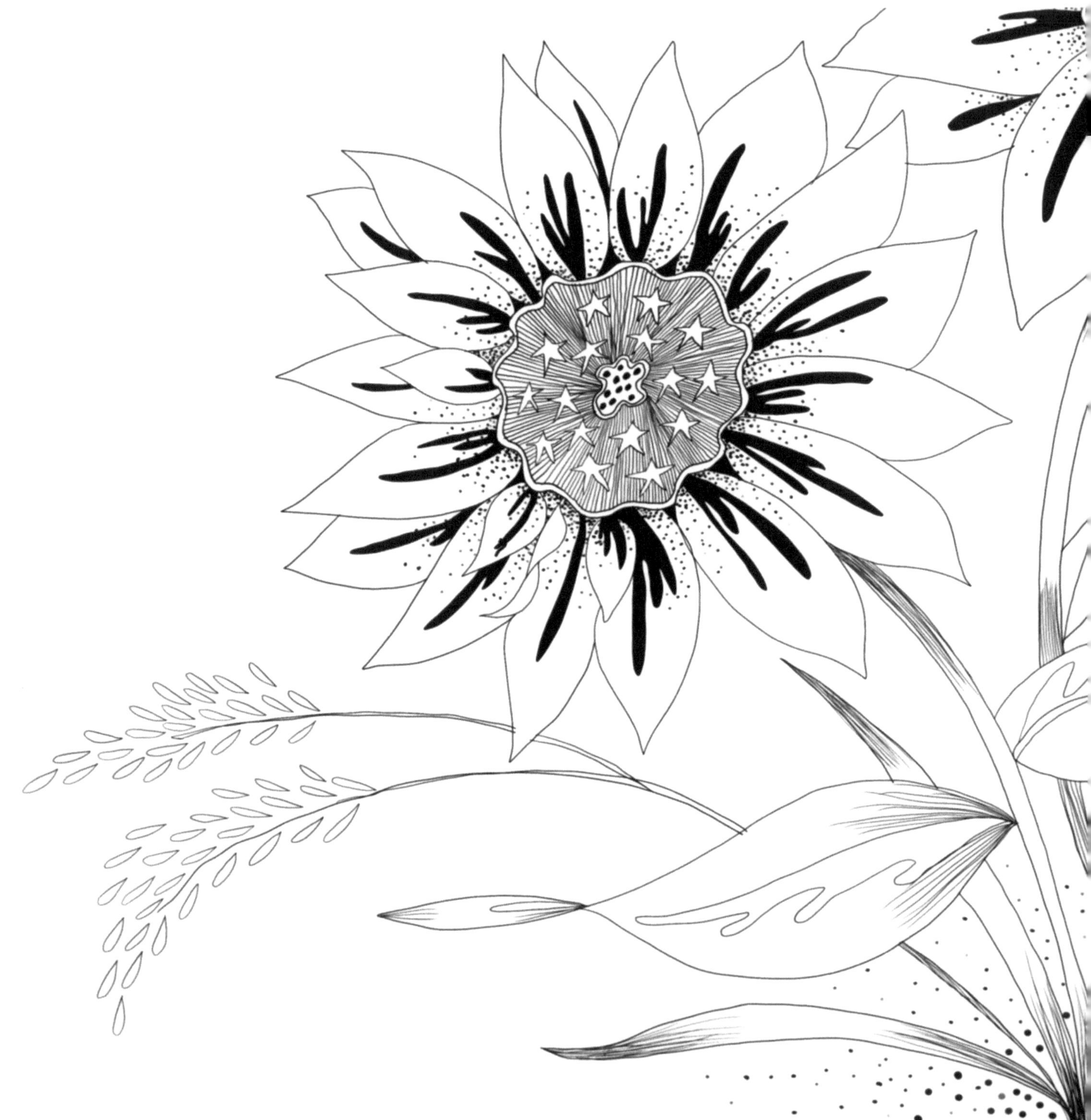

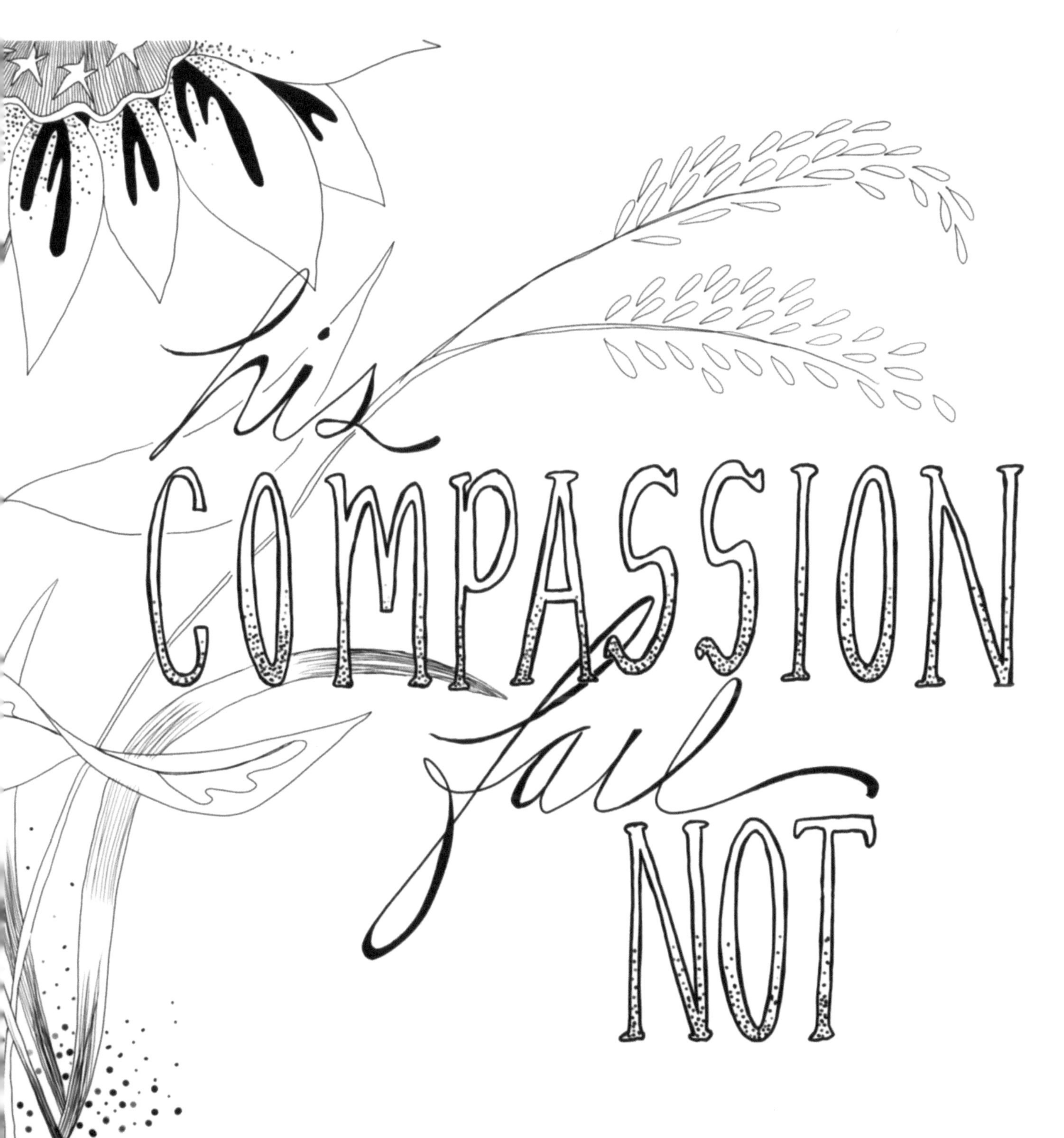

his
COMPASSION
fail
NOT

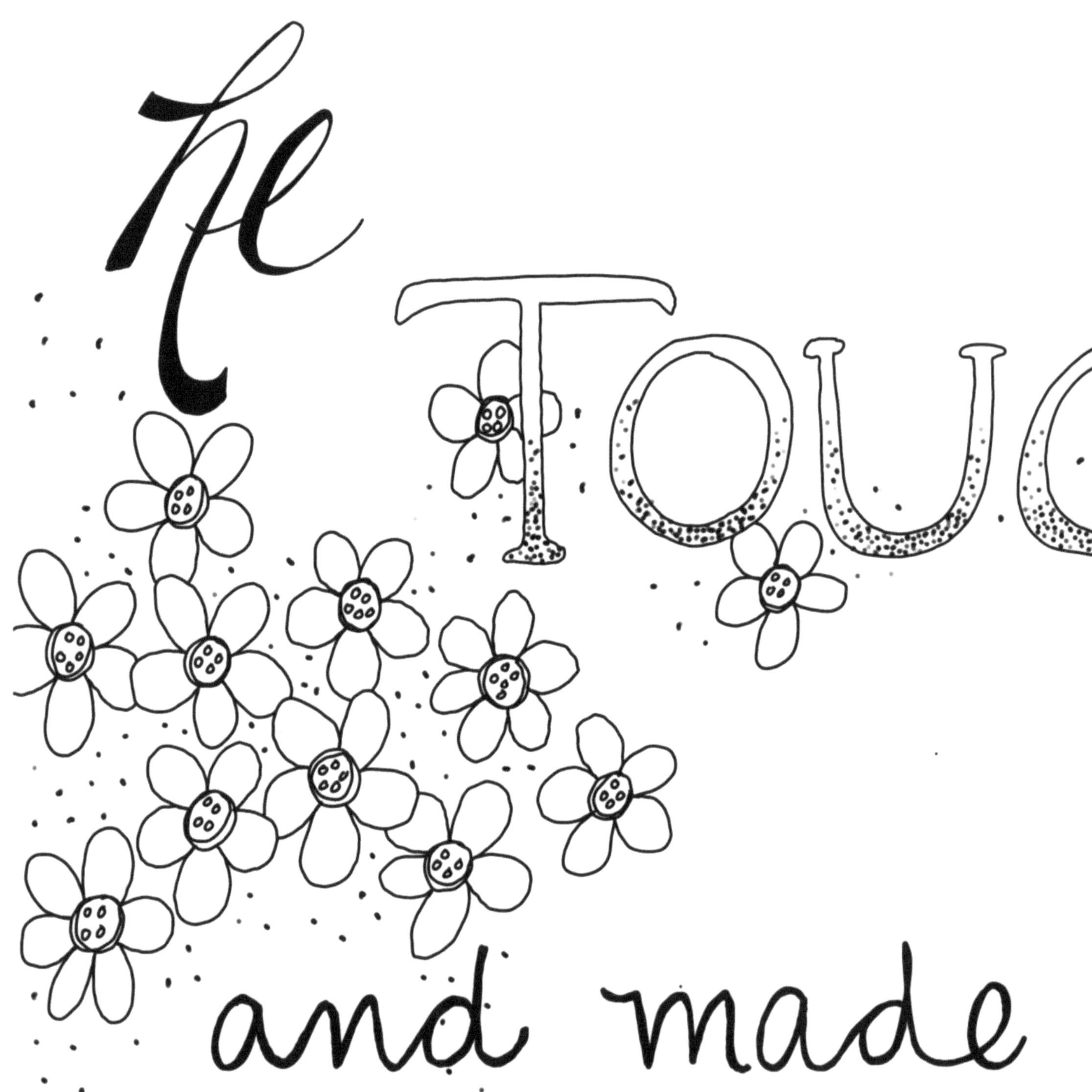

He Touched
and made

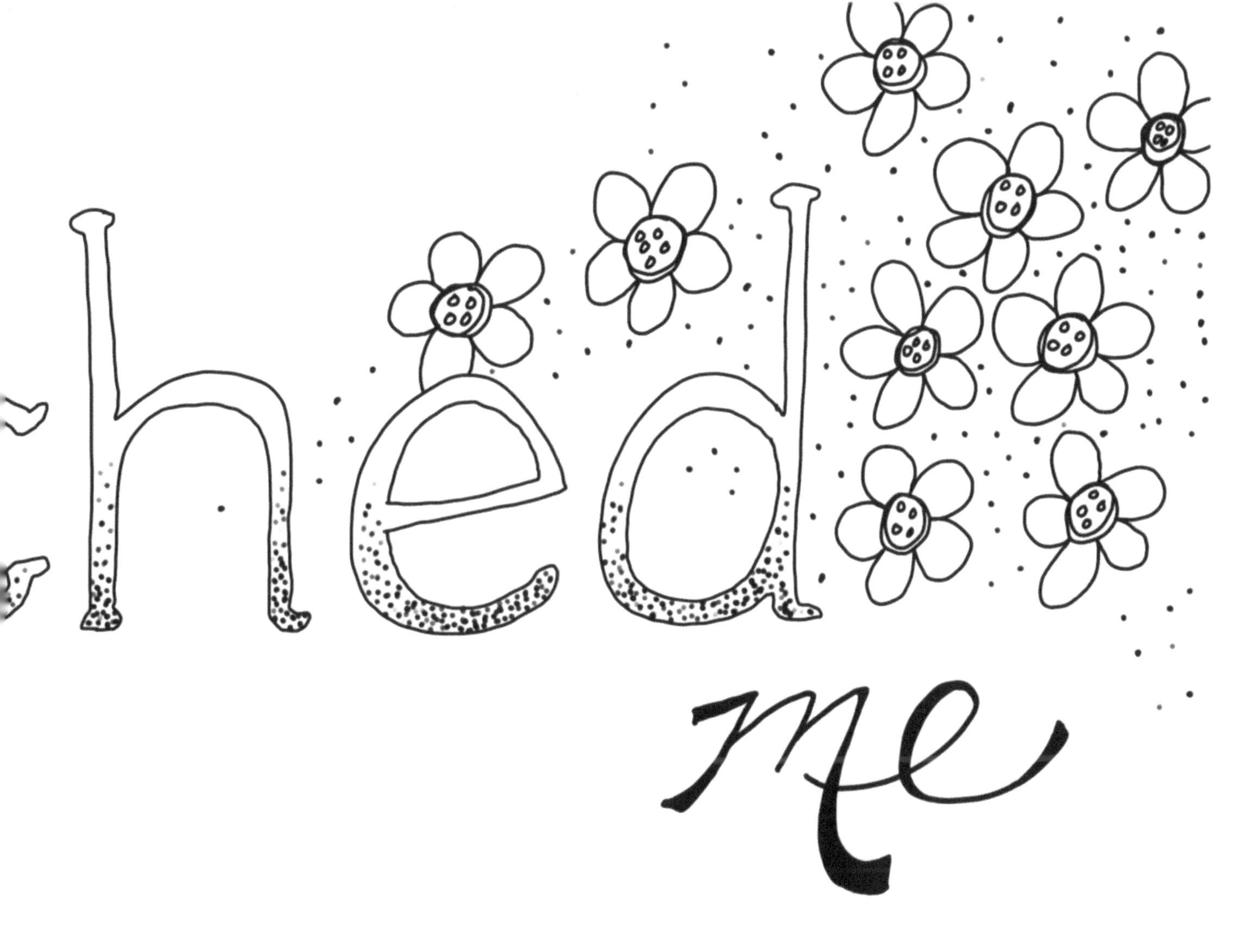

hed
me
me whole...

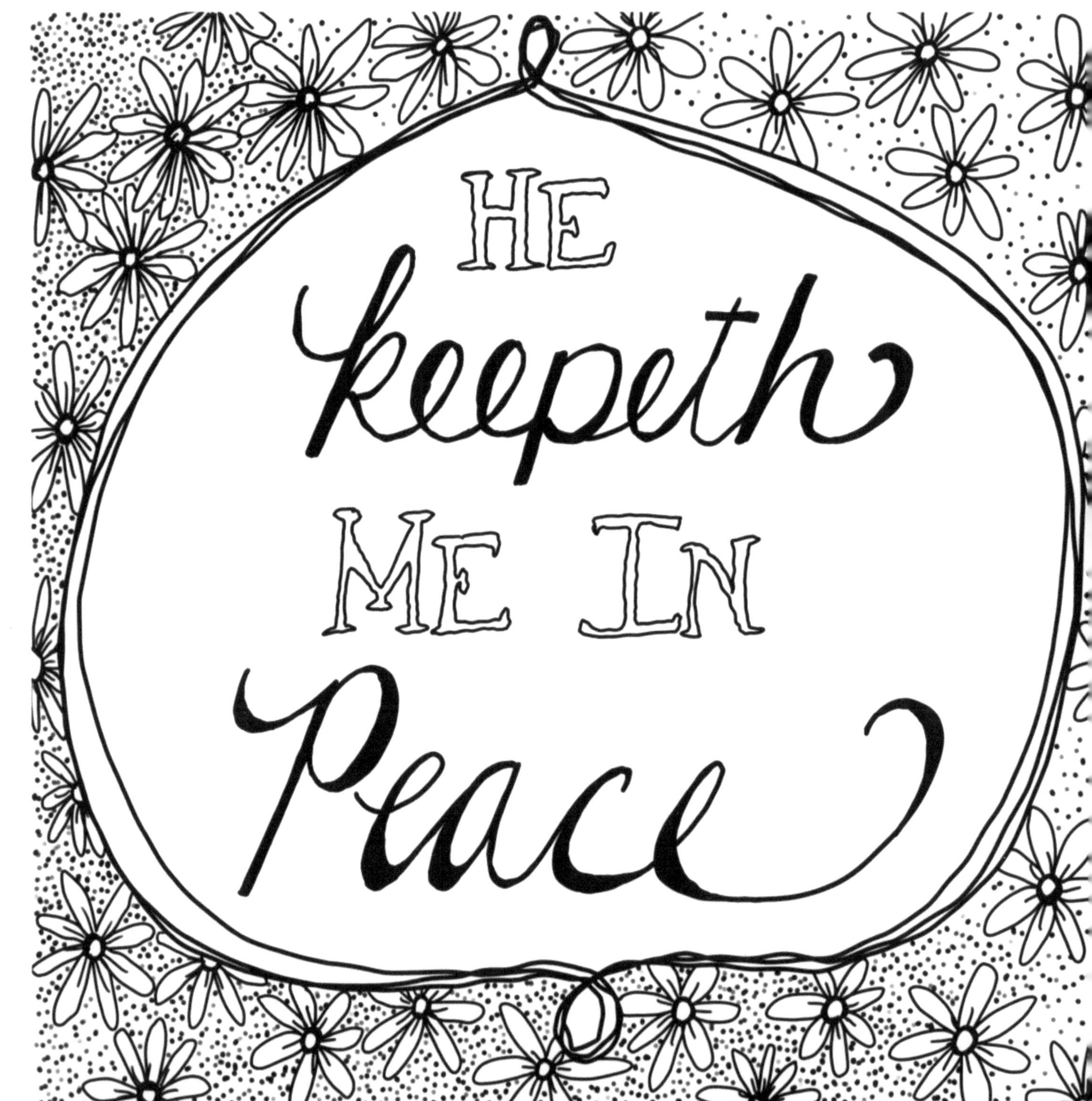

HE
keepeth
ME IN
Peace

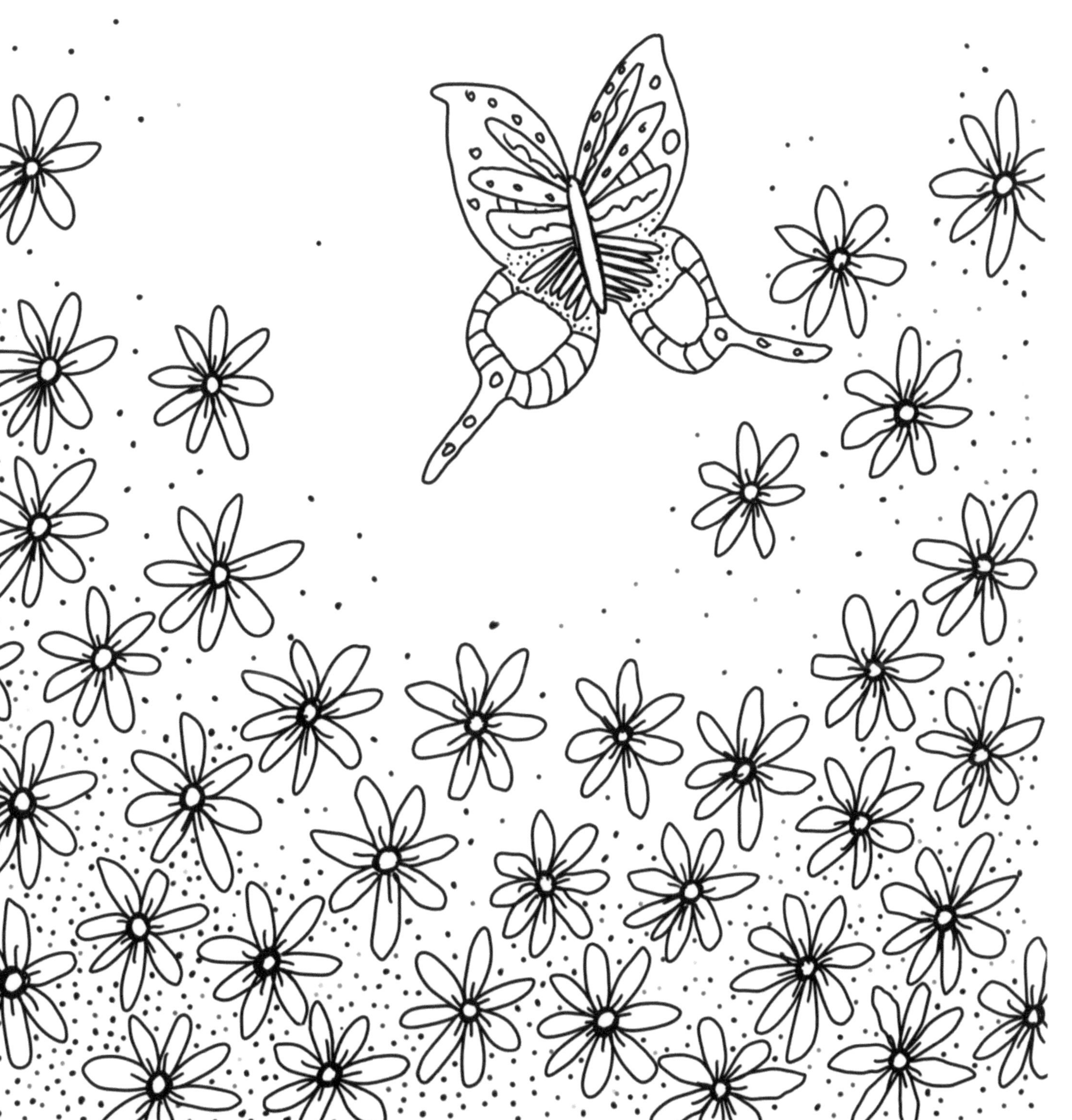

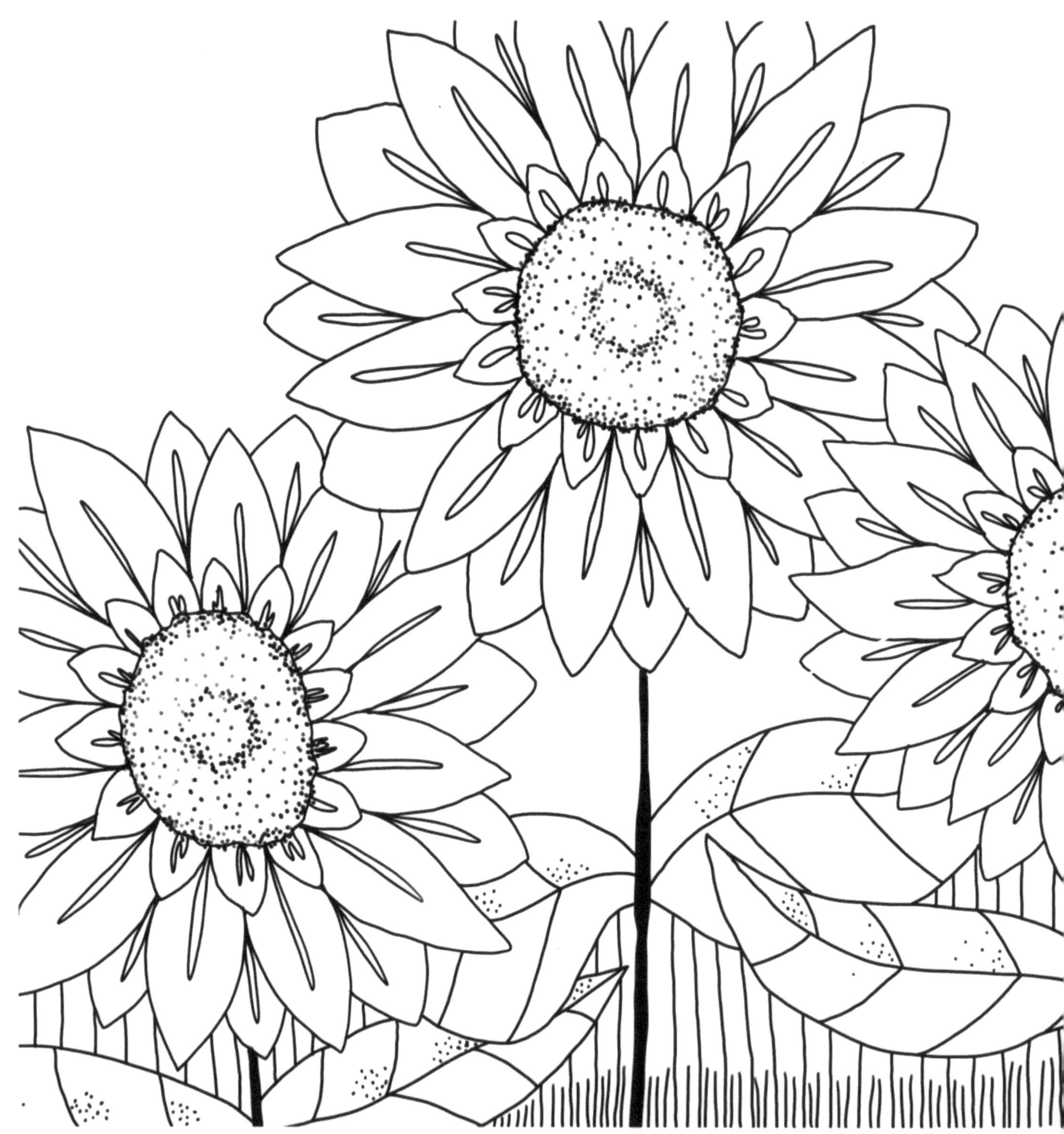

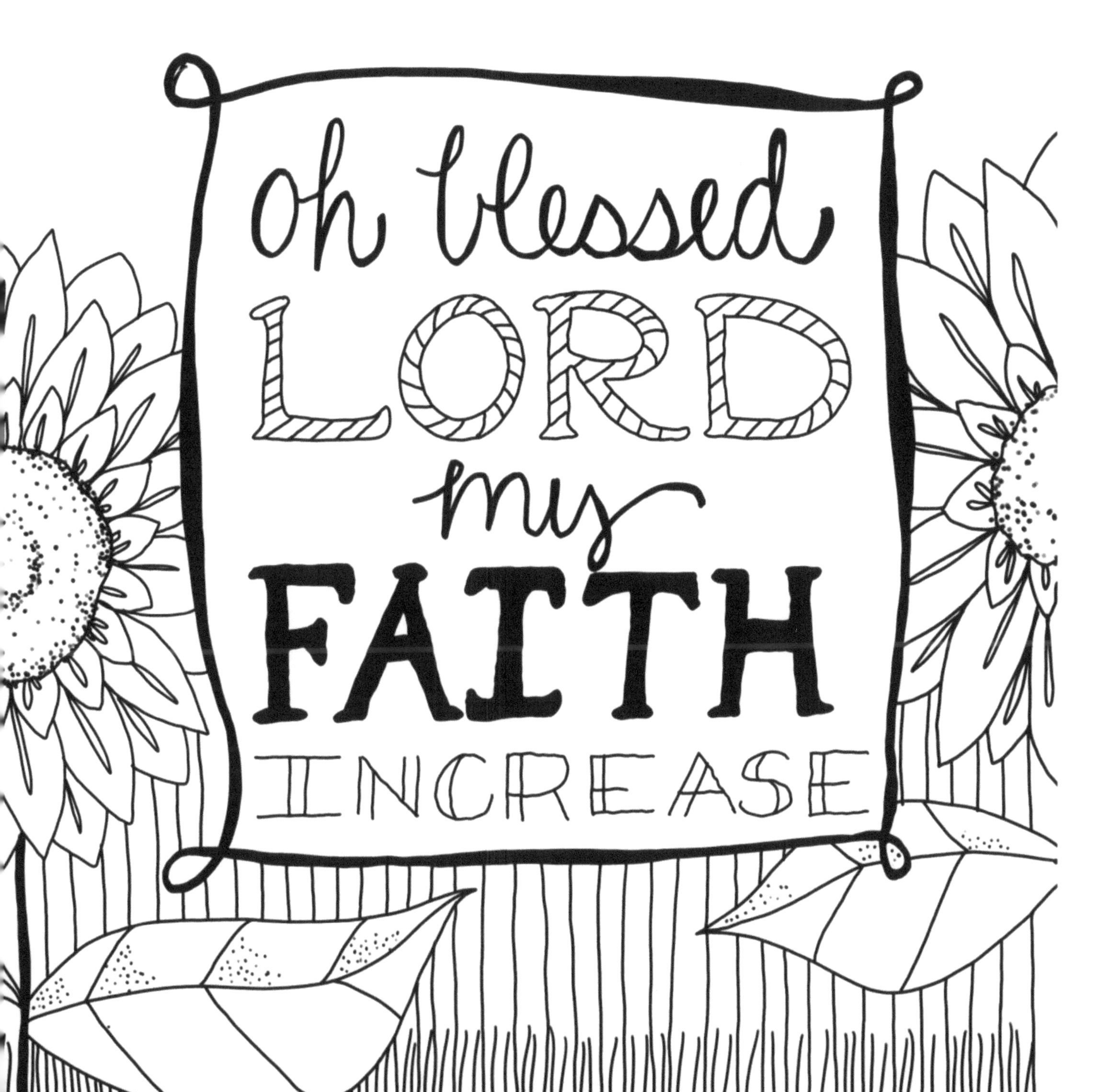

oh blessed
LORD
my
FAITH
INCREASE

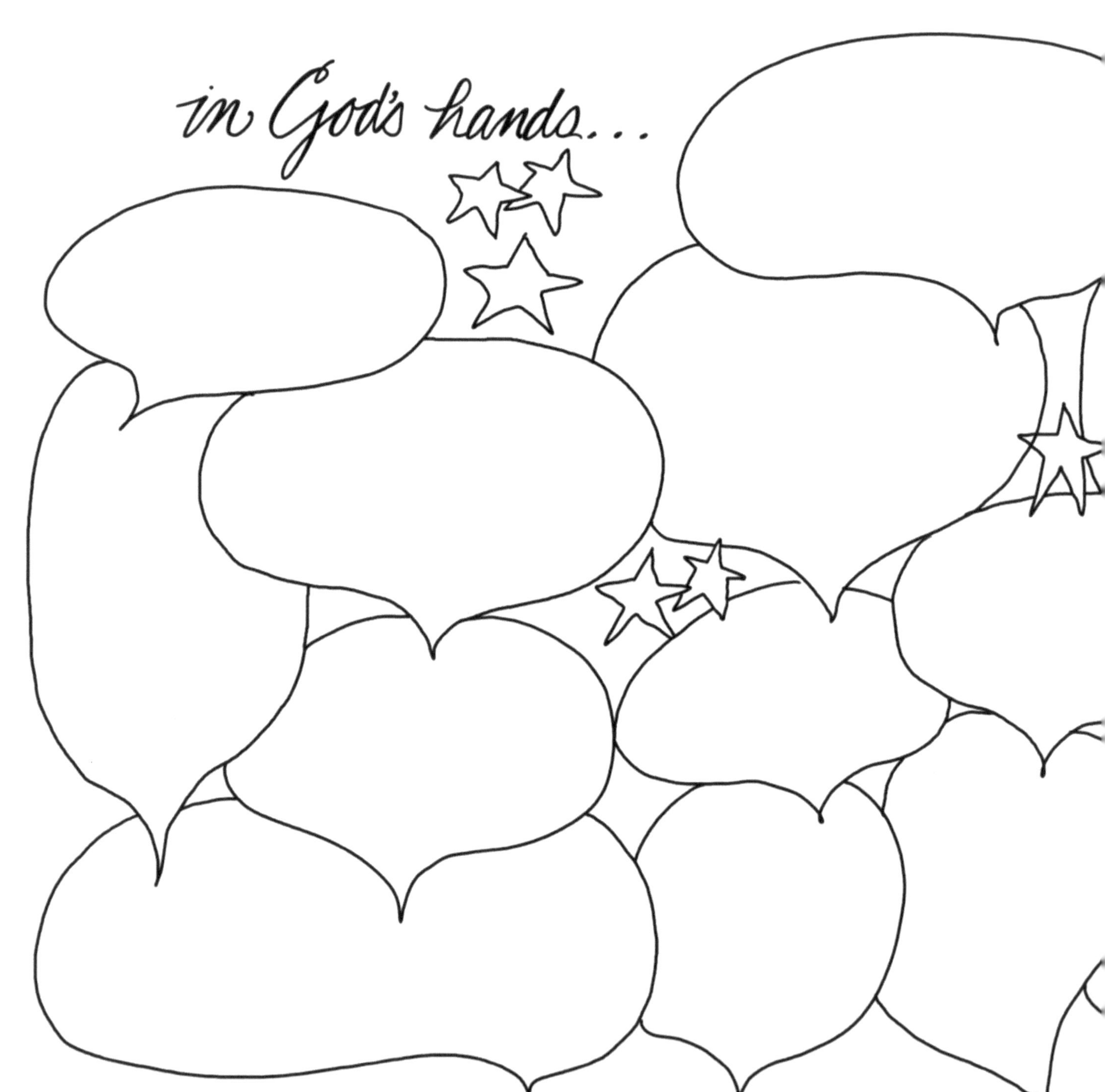
in God's hands...

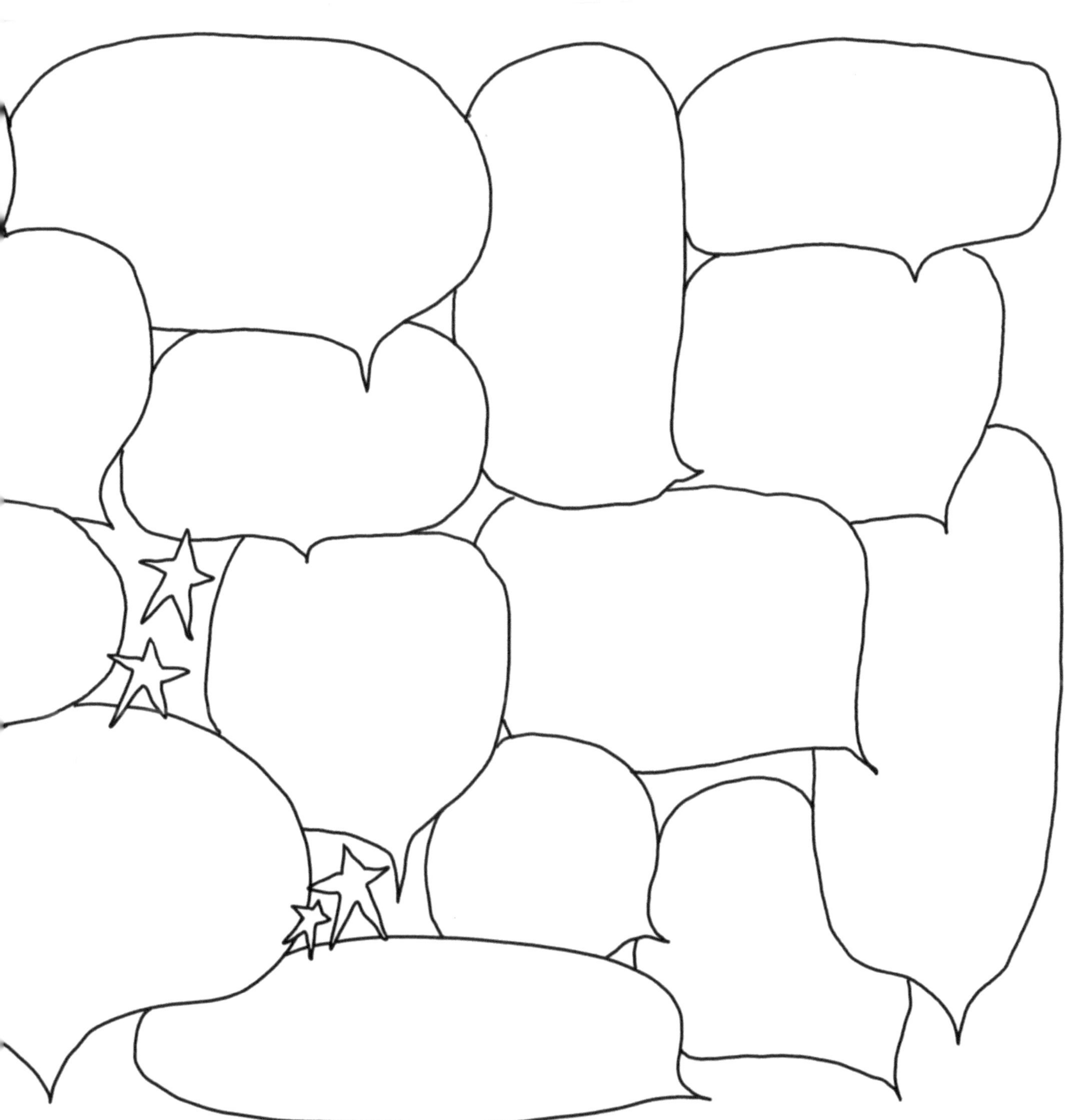

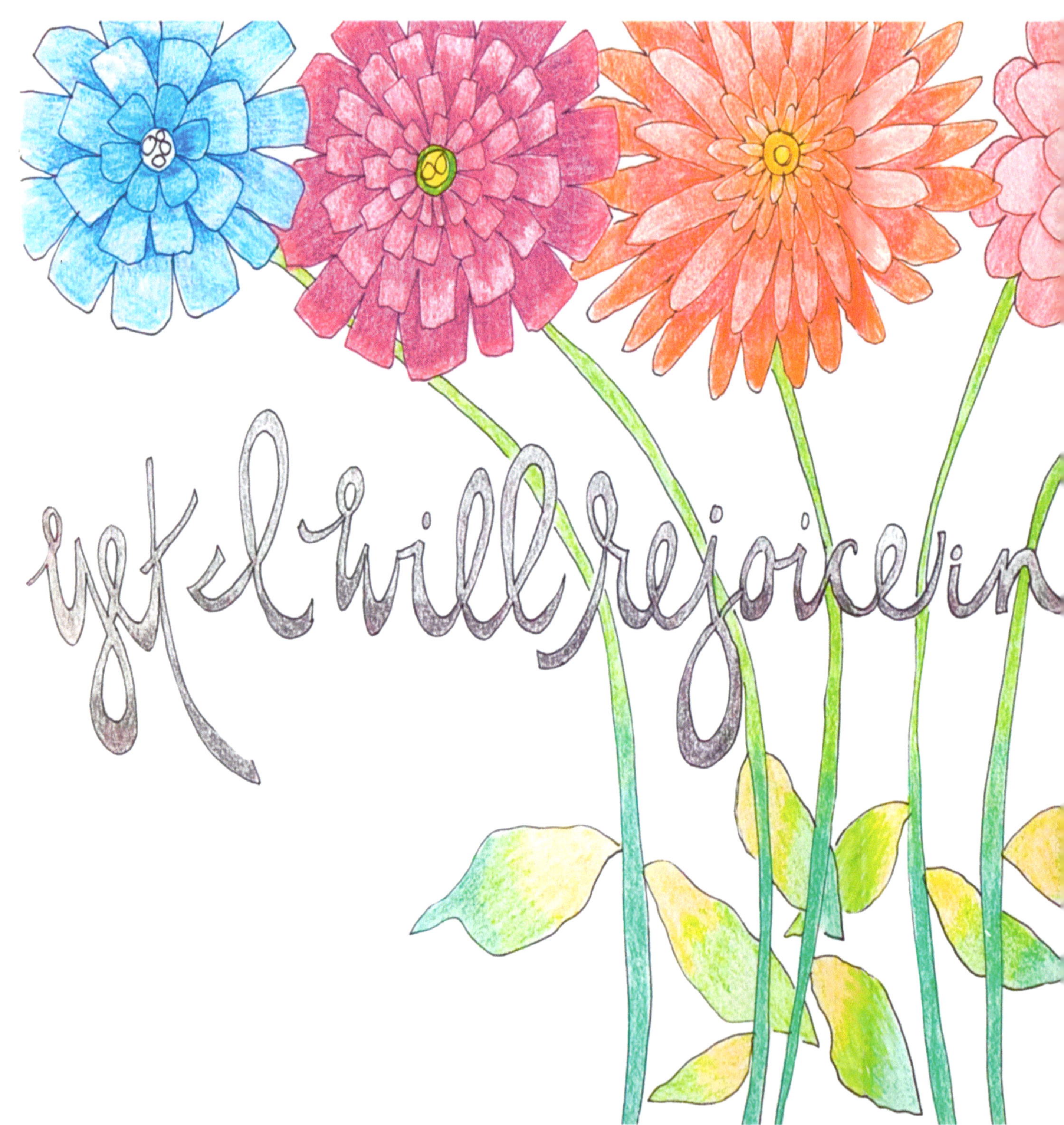
yet I will rejoice in

the Lord
HAB 3:17-18

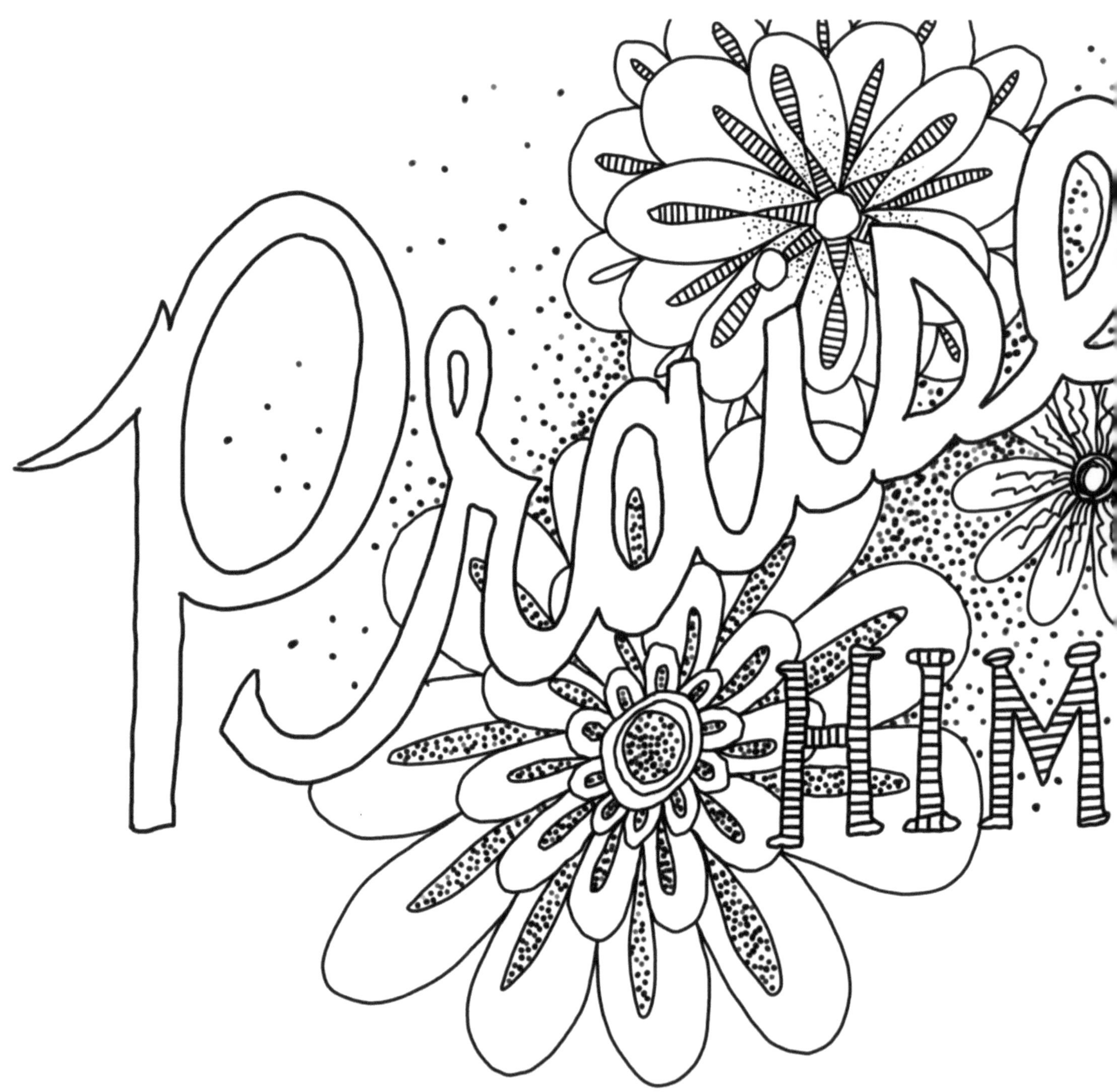

Praise
HIM

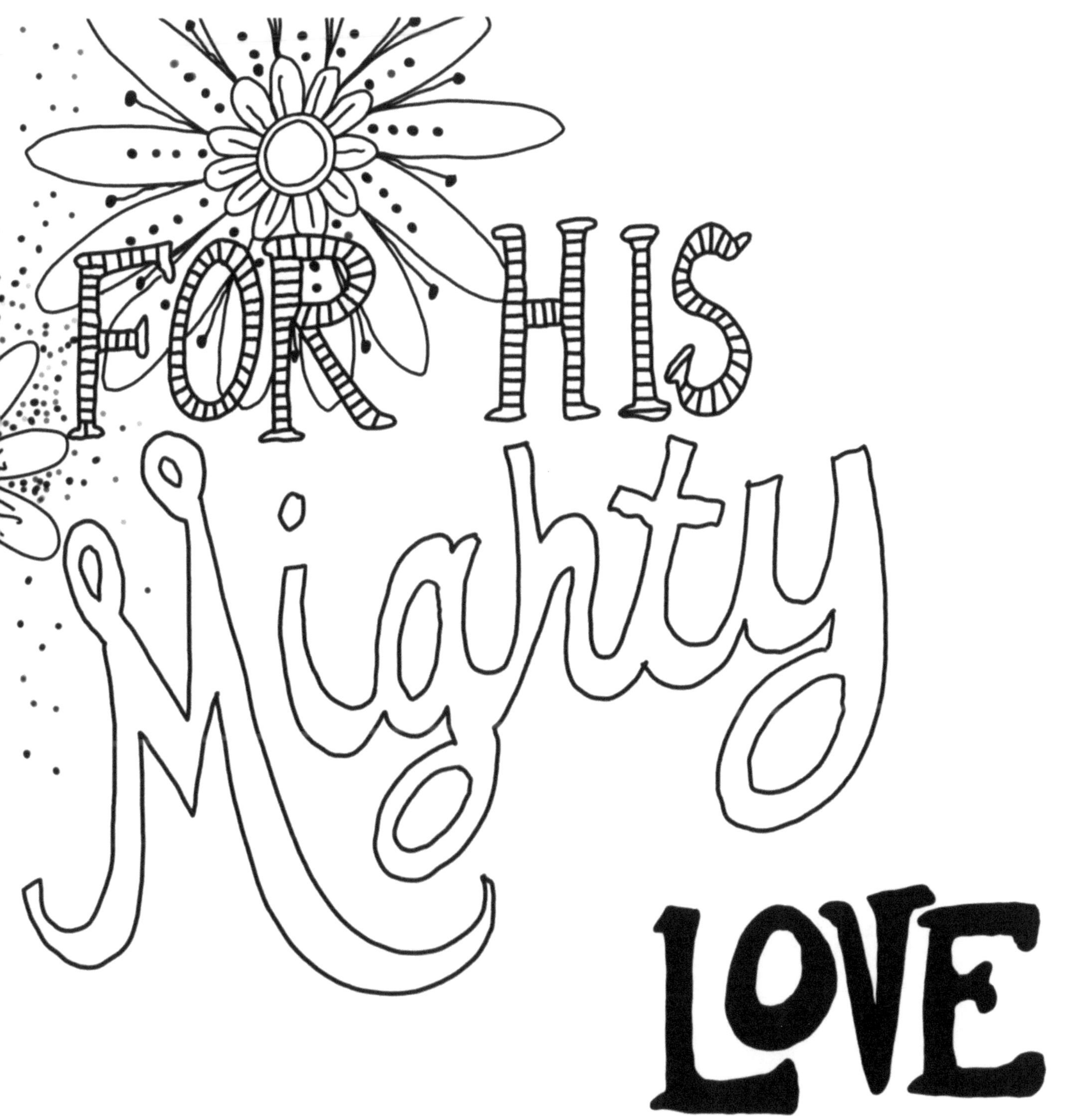

FOR HIS
Mighty
LOVE

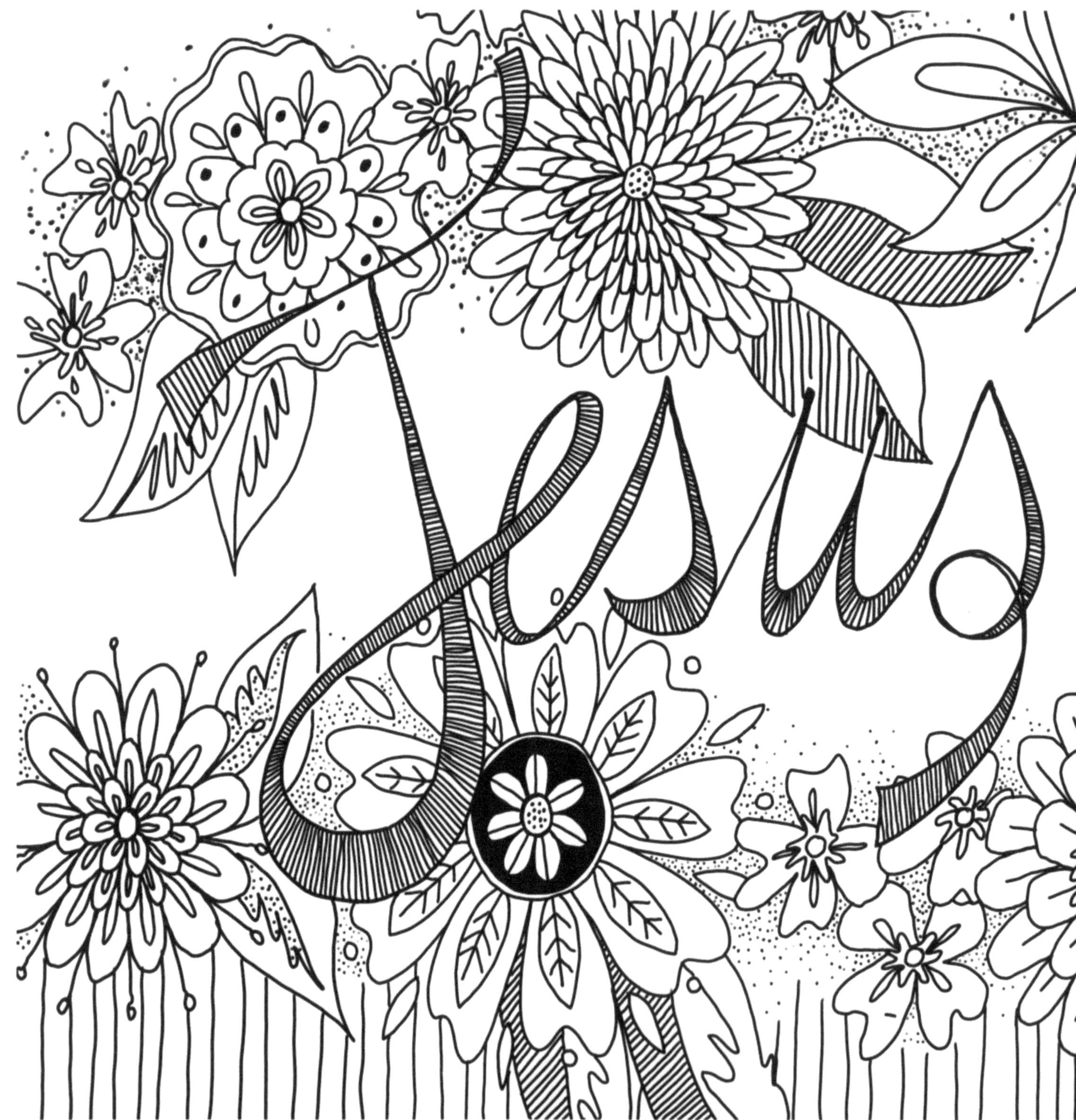
Jesus

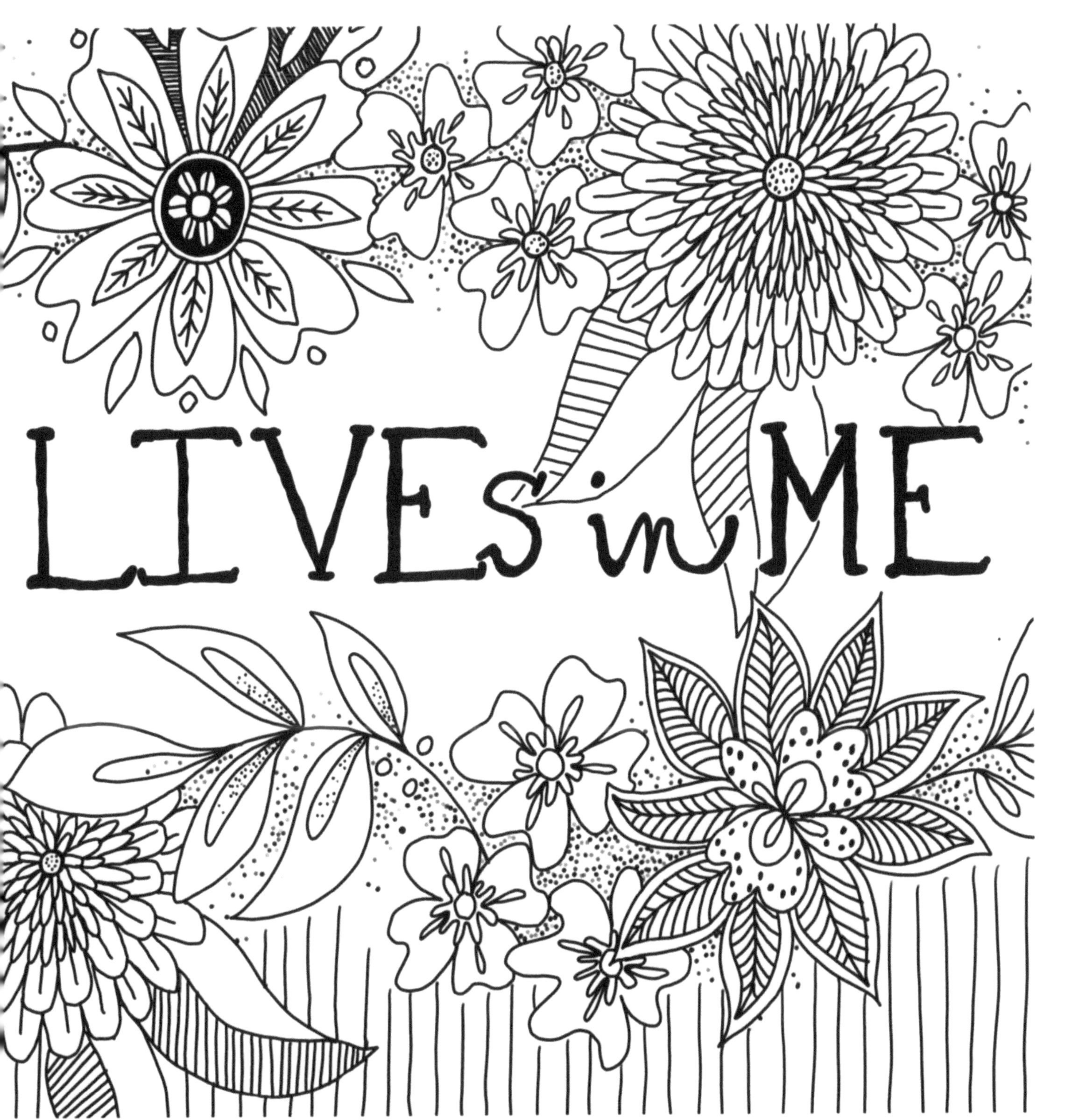

LIVES in ME

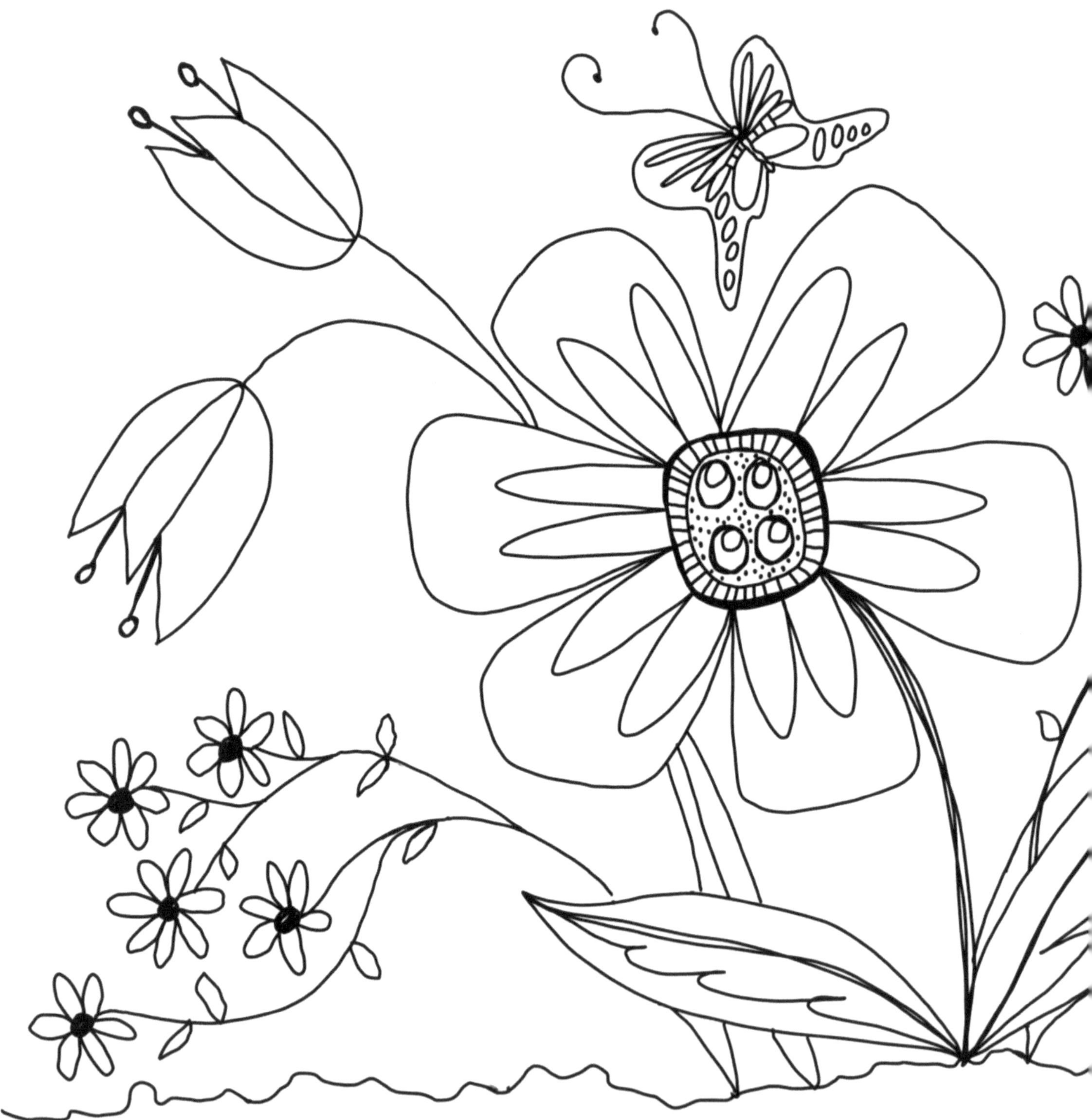

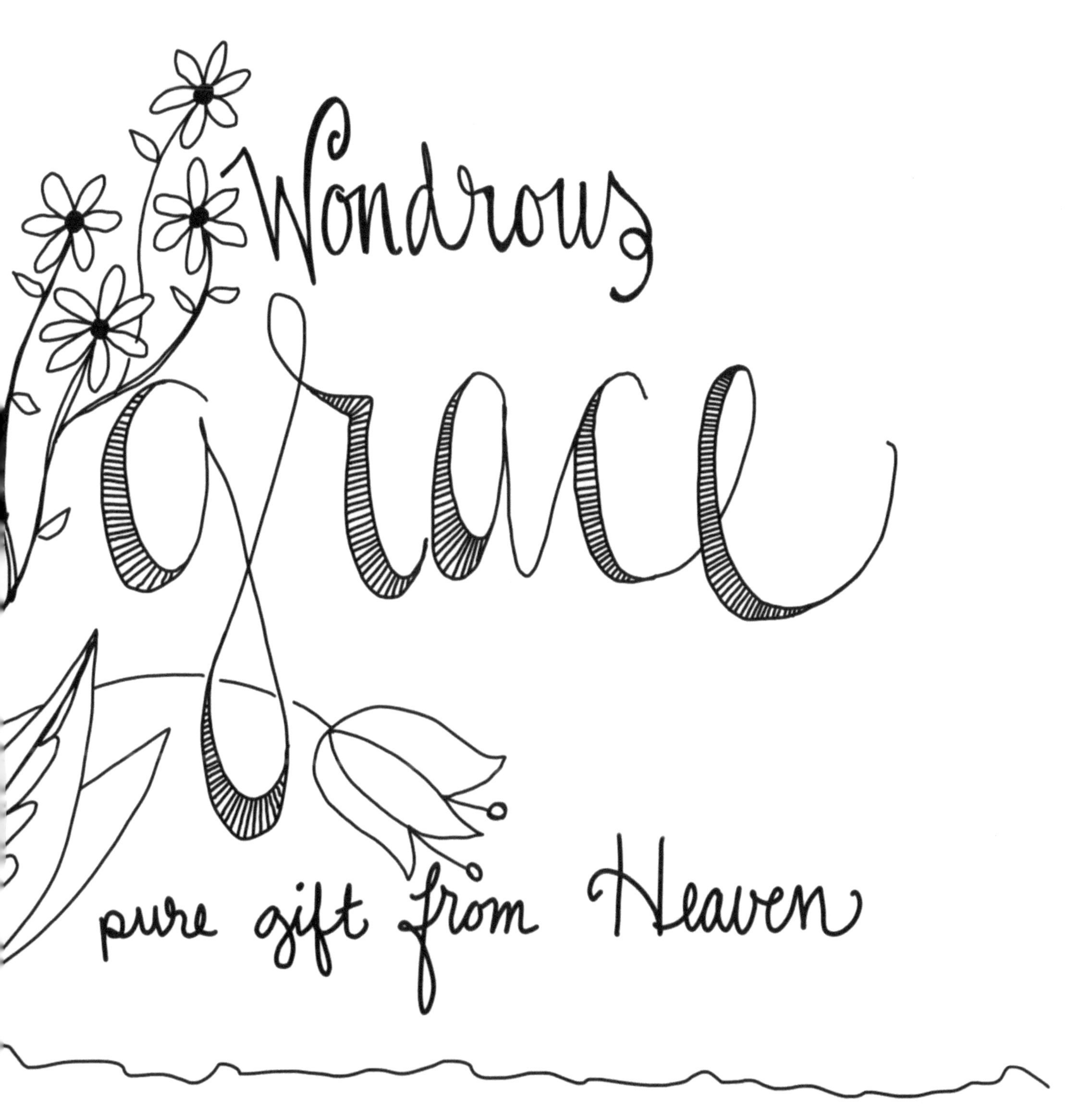

Wondrous
grace
pure gift from Heaven

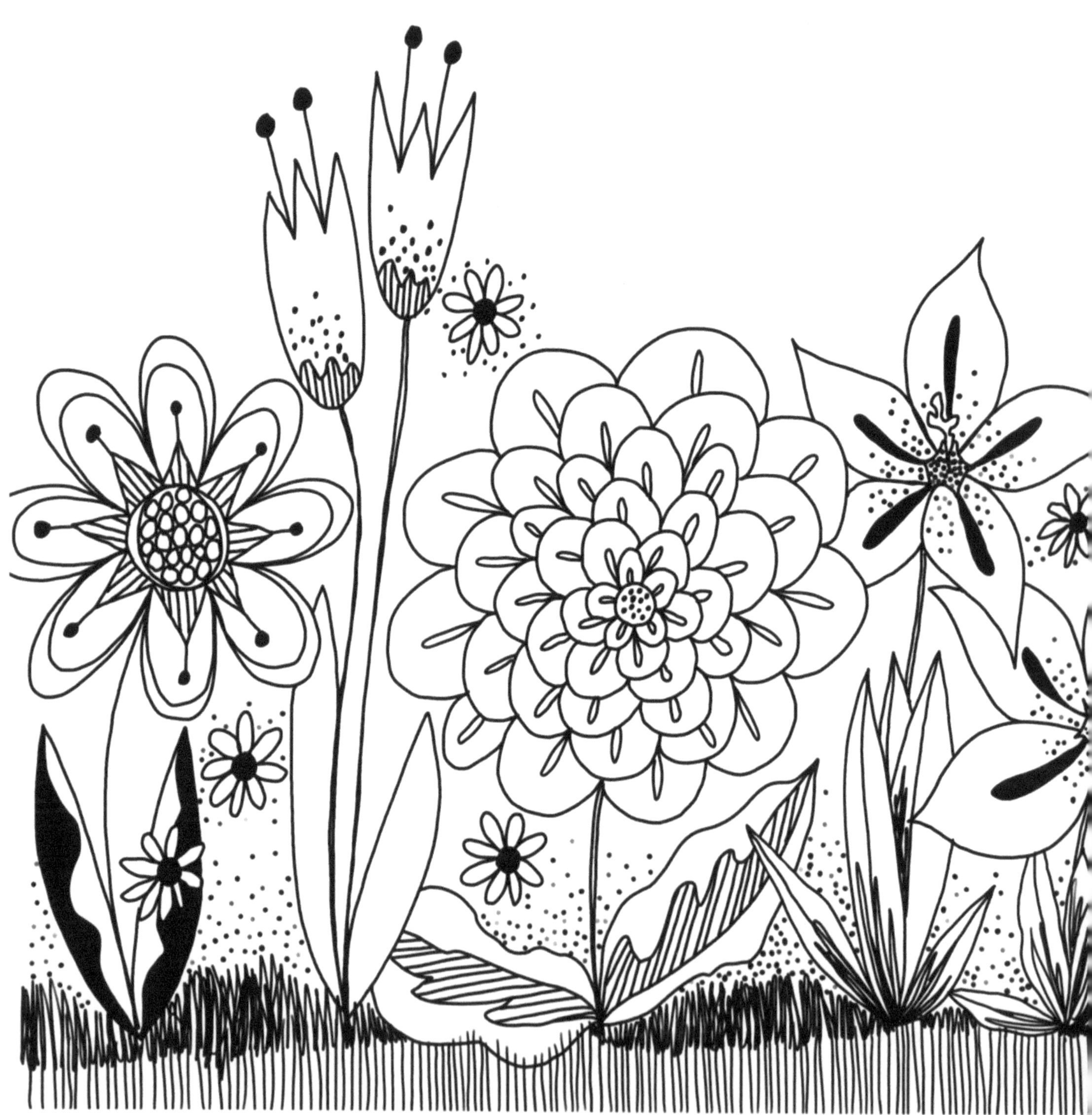

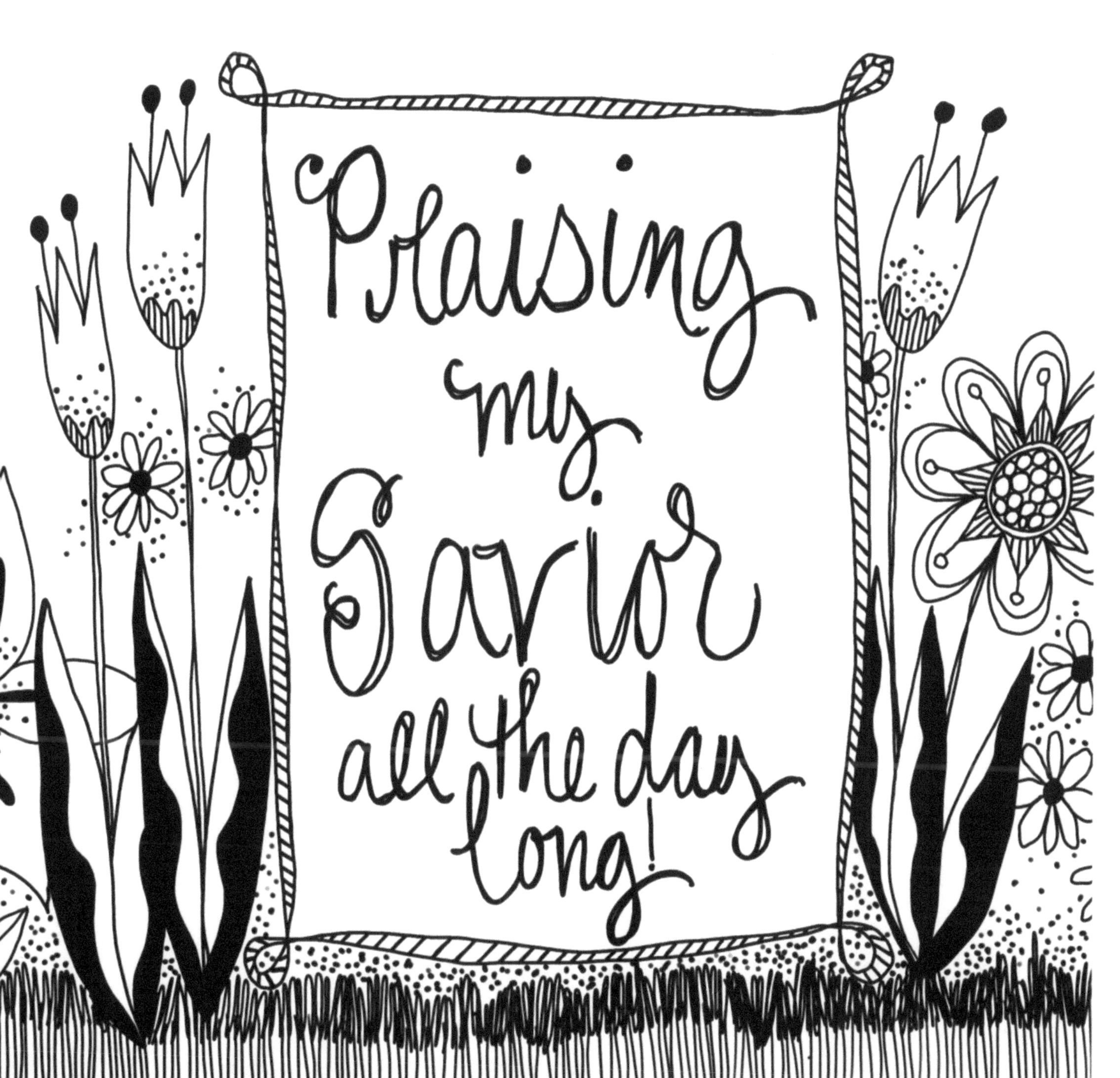

Praising my Savior all the day long!

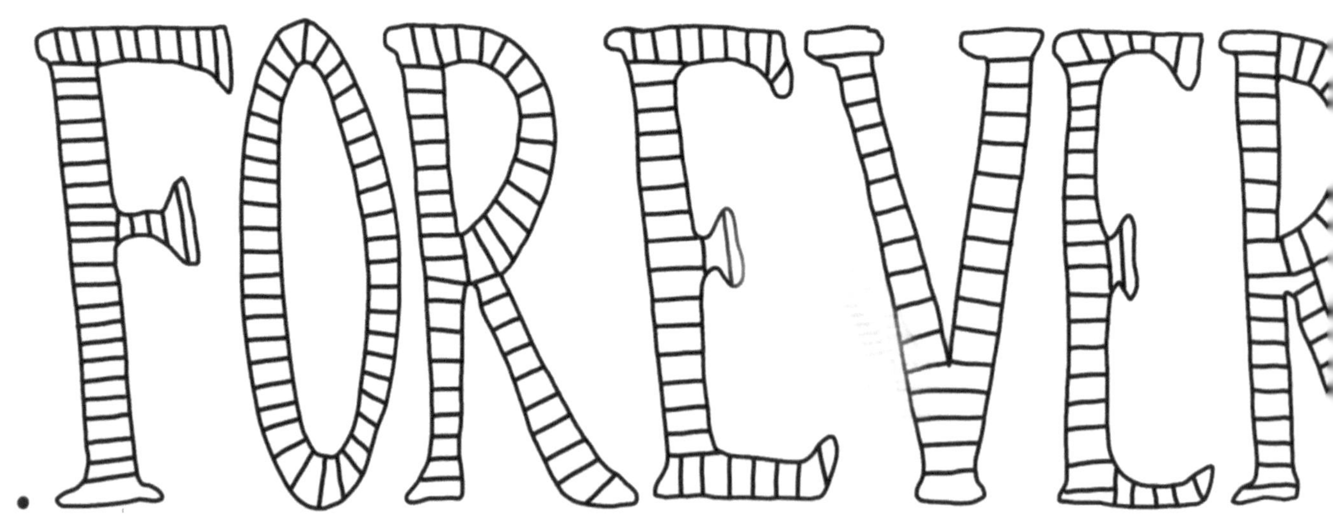

GOD,
I will be thine
FOREVER

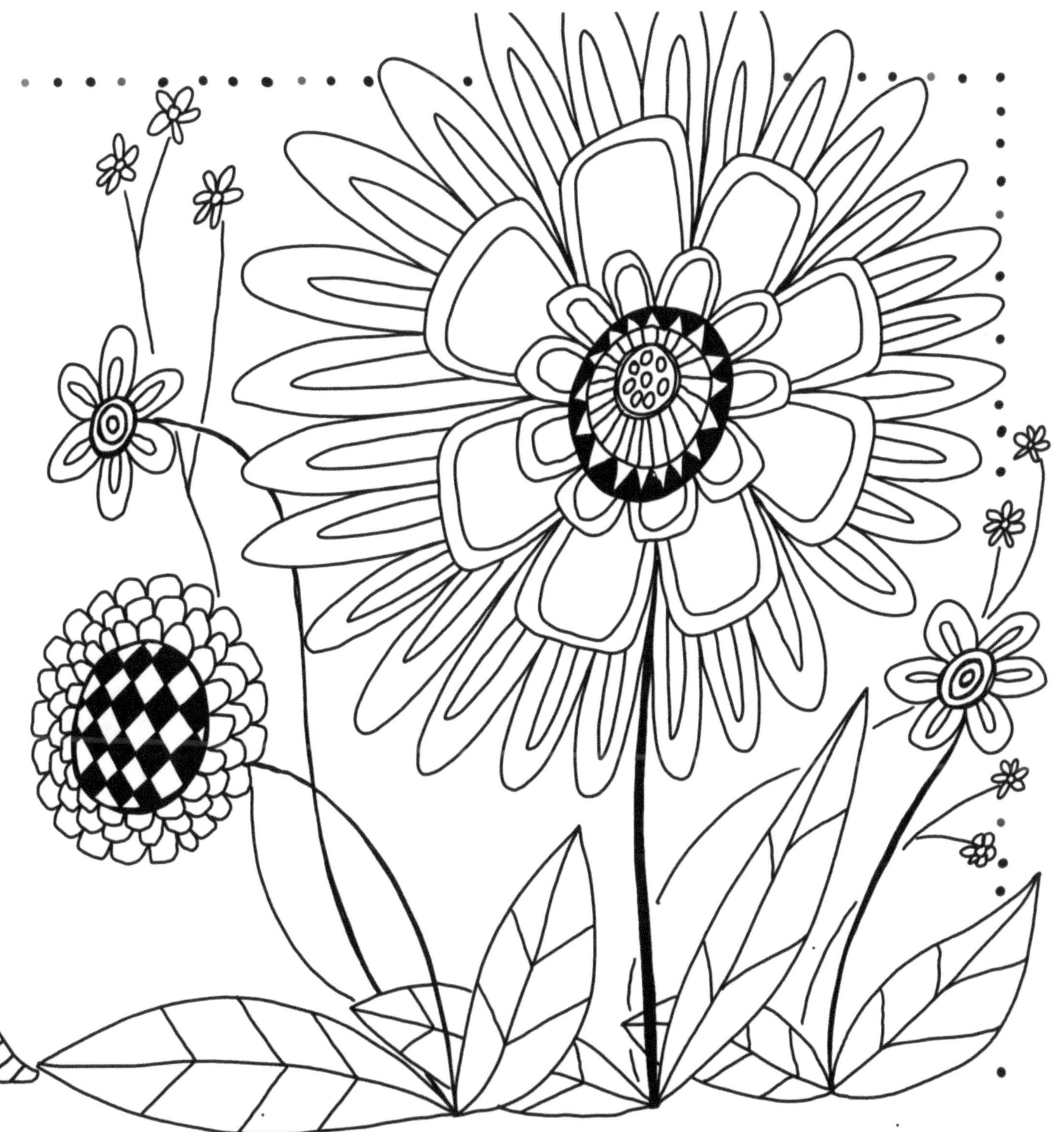

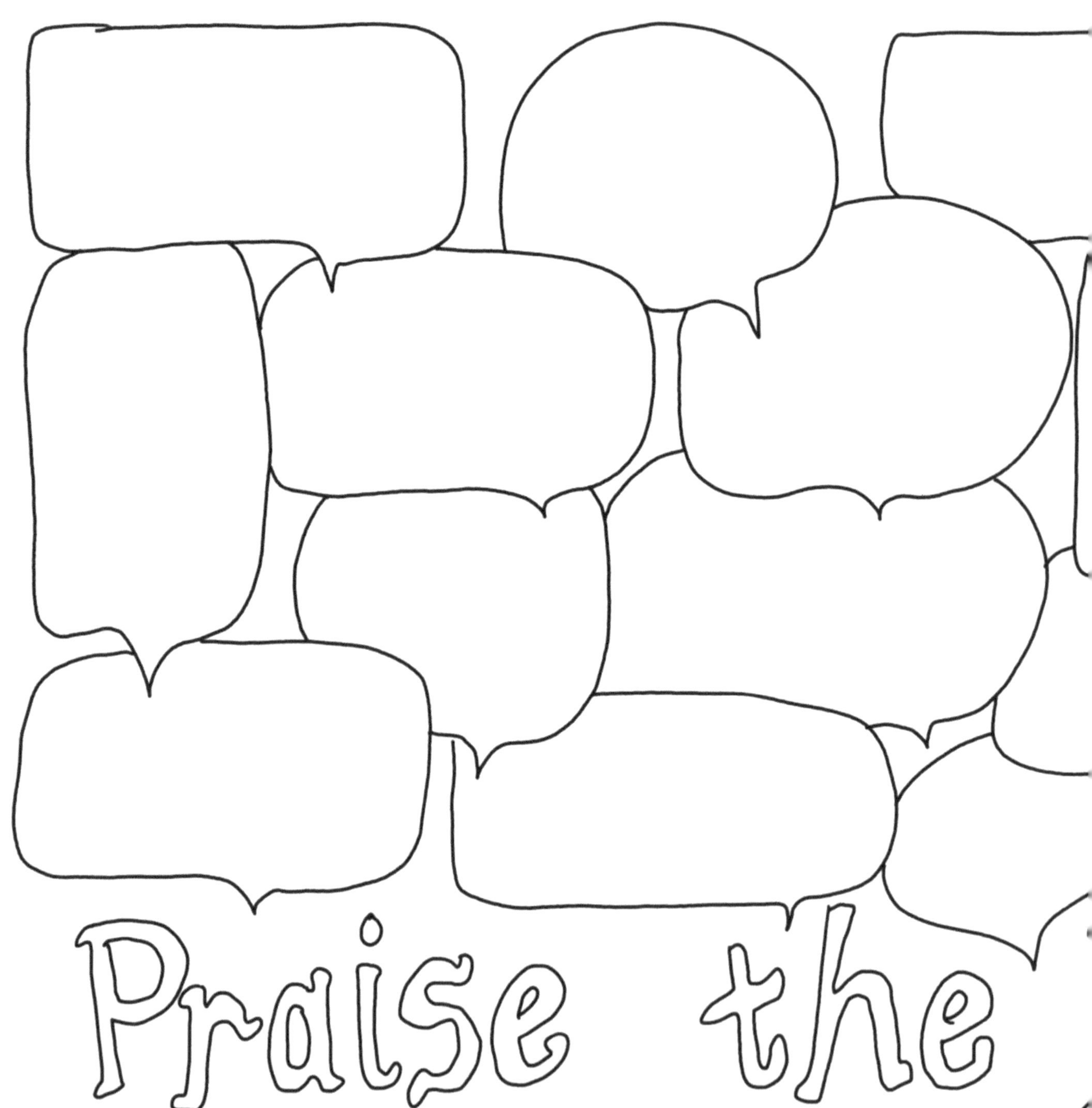

Praise the

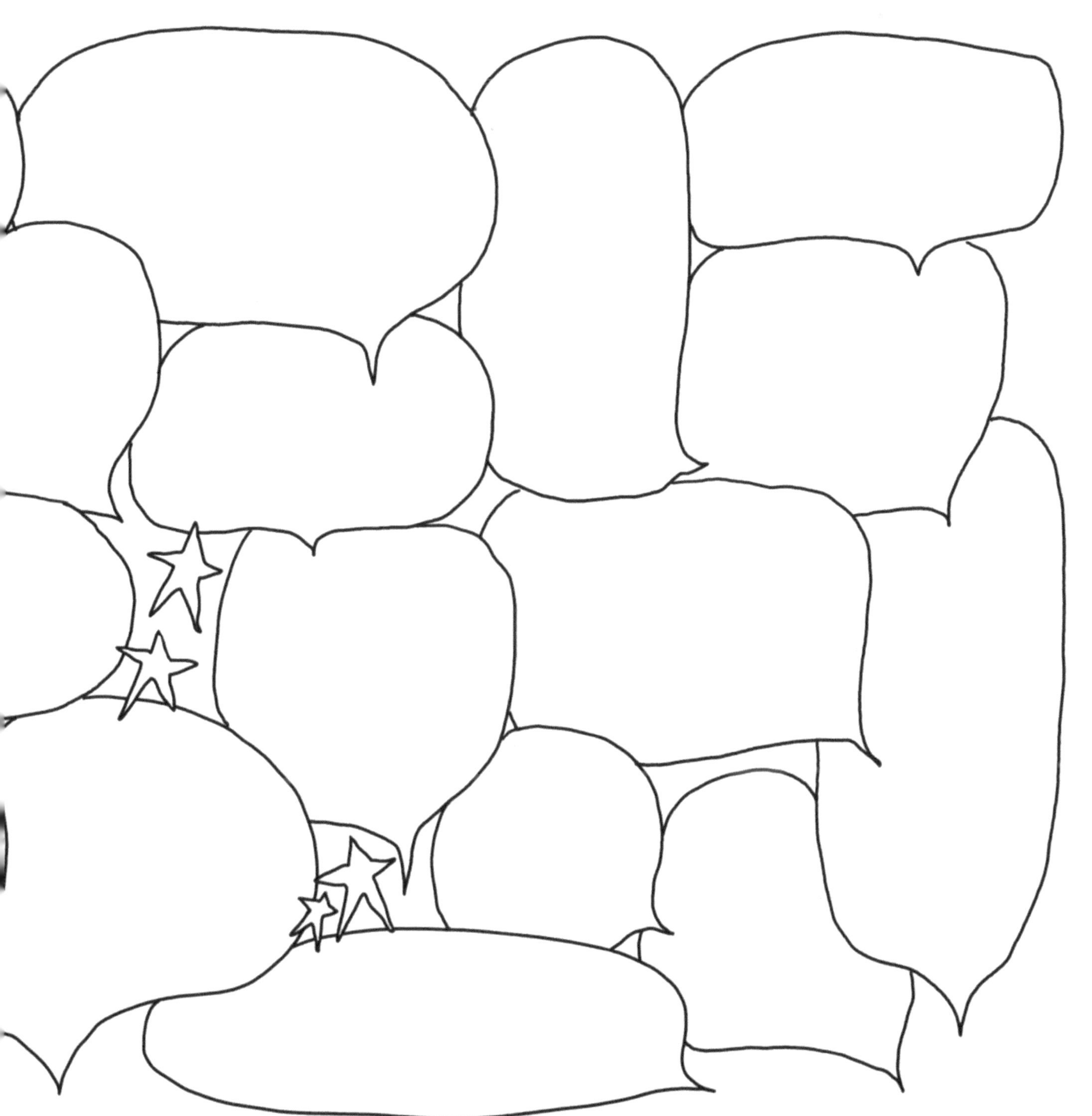

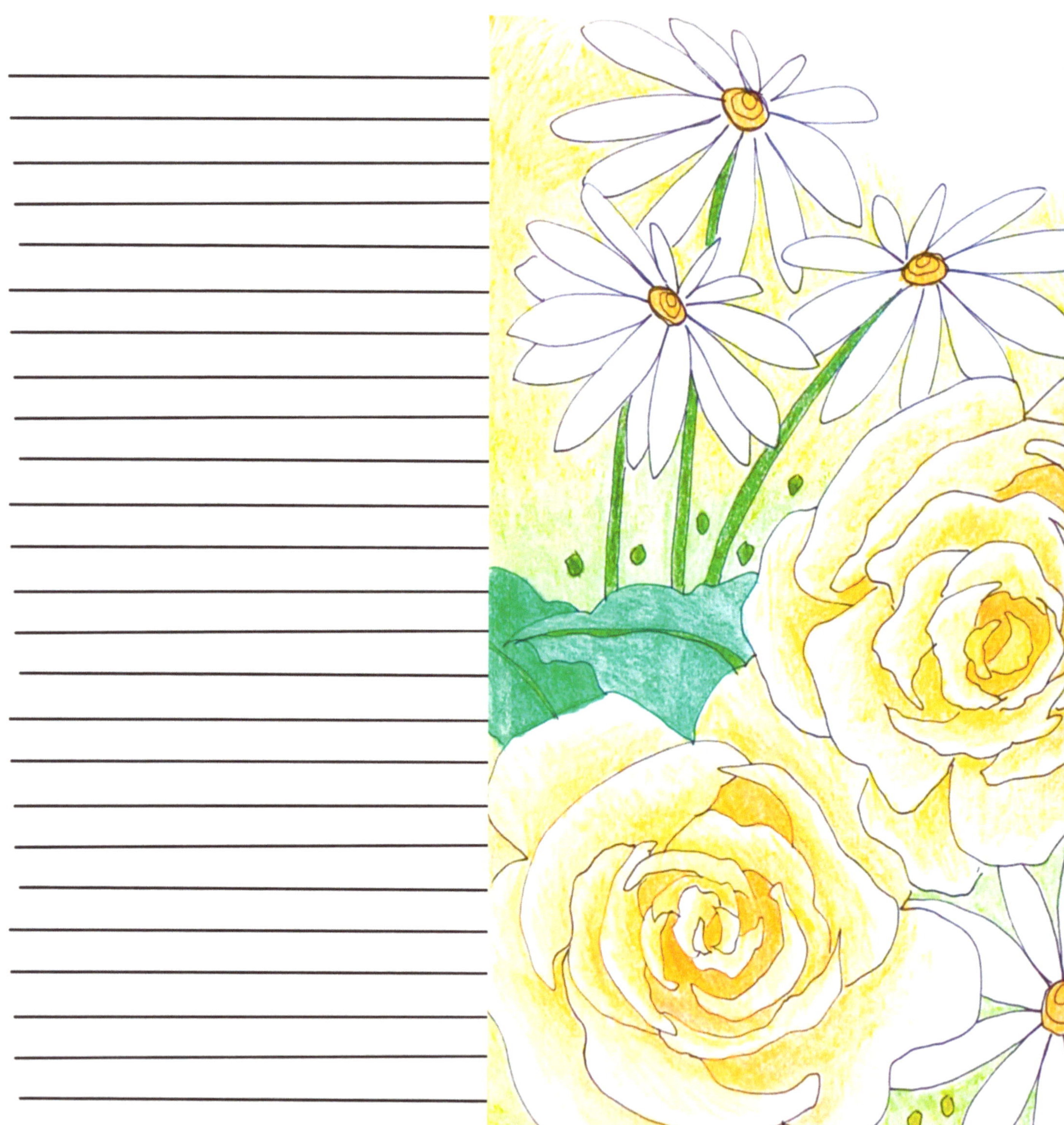

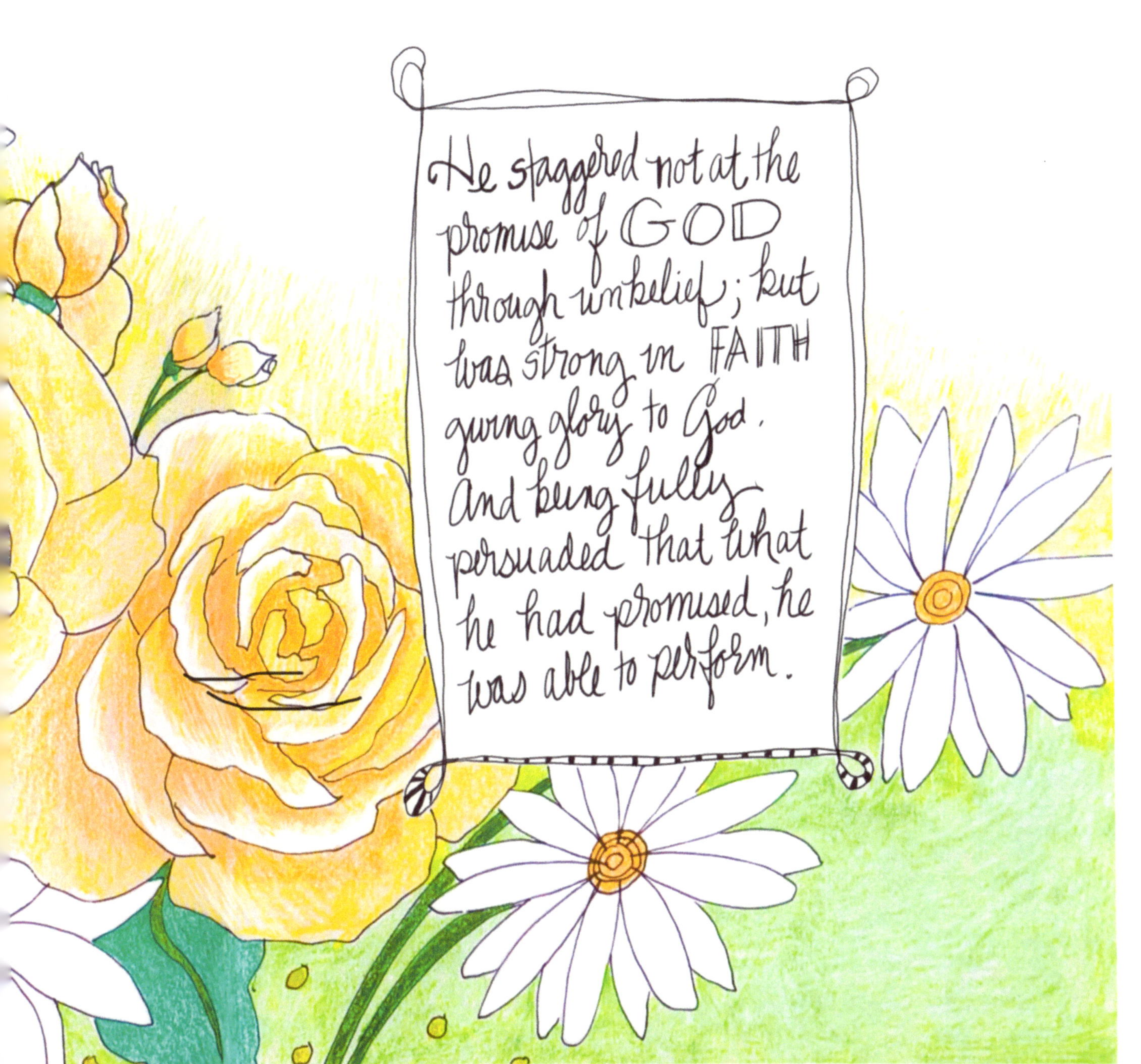
He staggered not at the promise of GOD through unbelief; but was strong in FAITH giving glory to God. And being fully persuaded that what he had promised, he was able to perform.

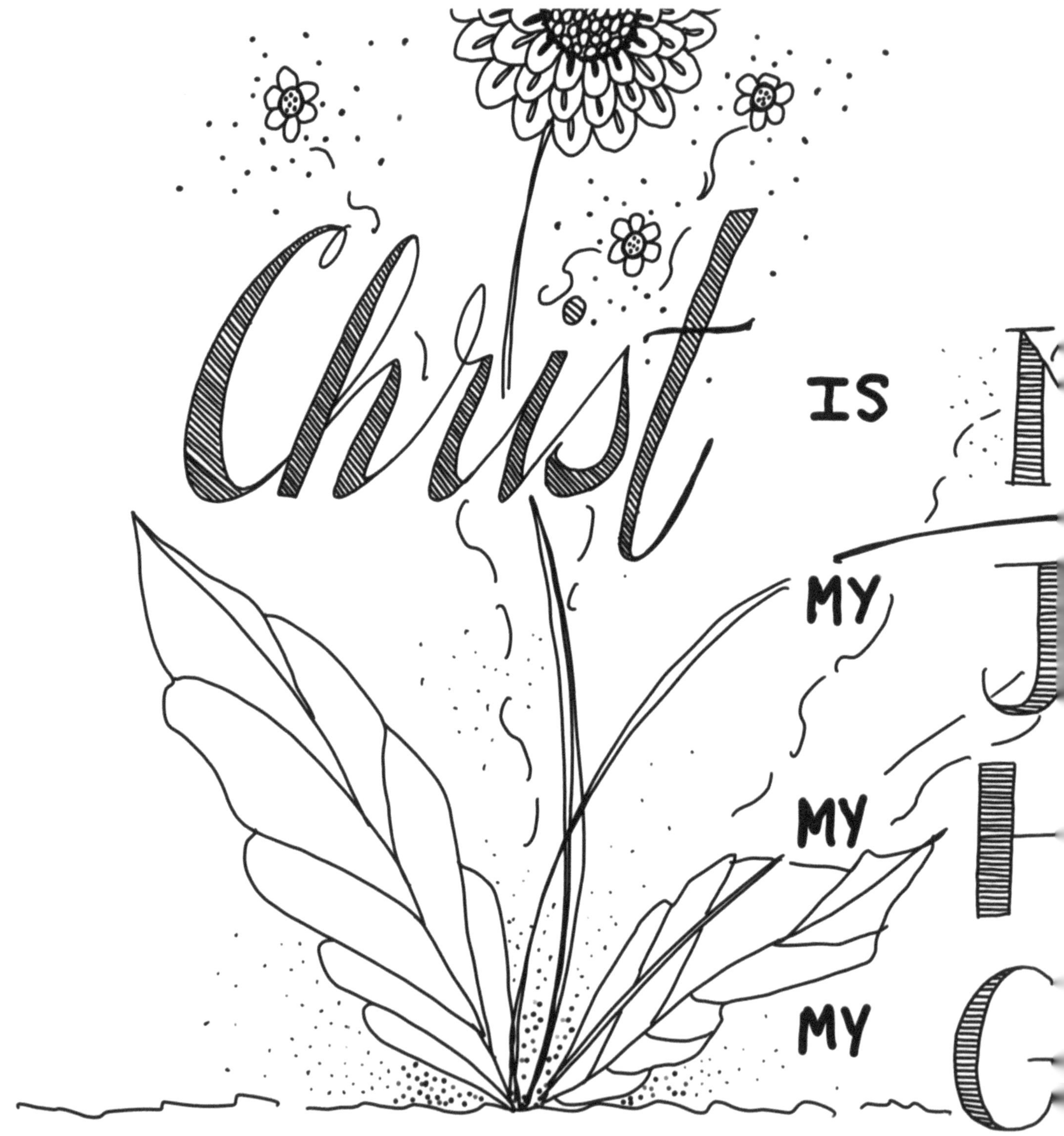

Christ
IS
MY
MY
MY

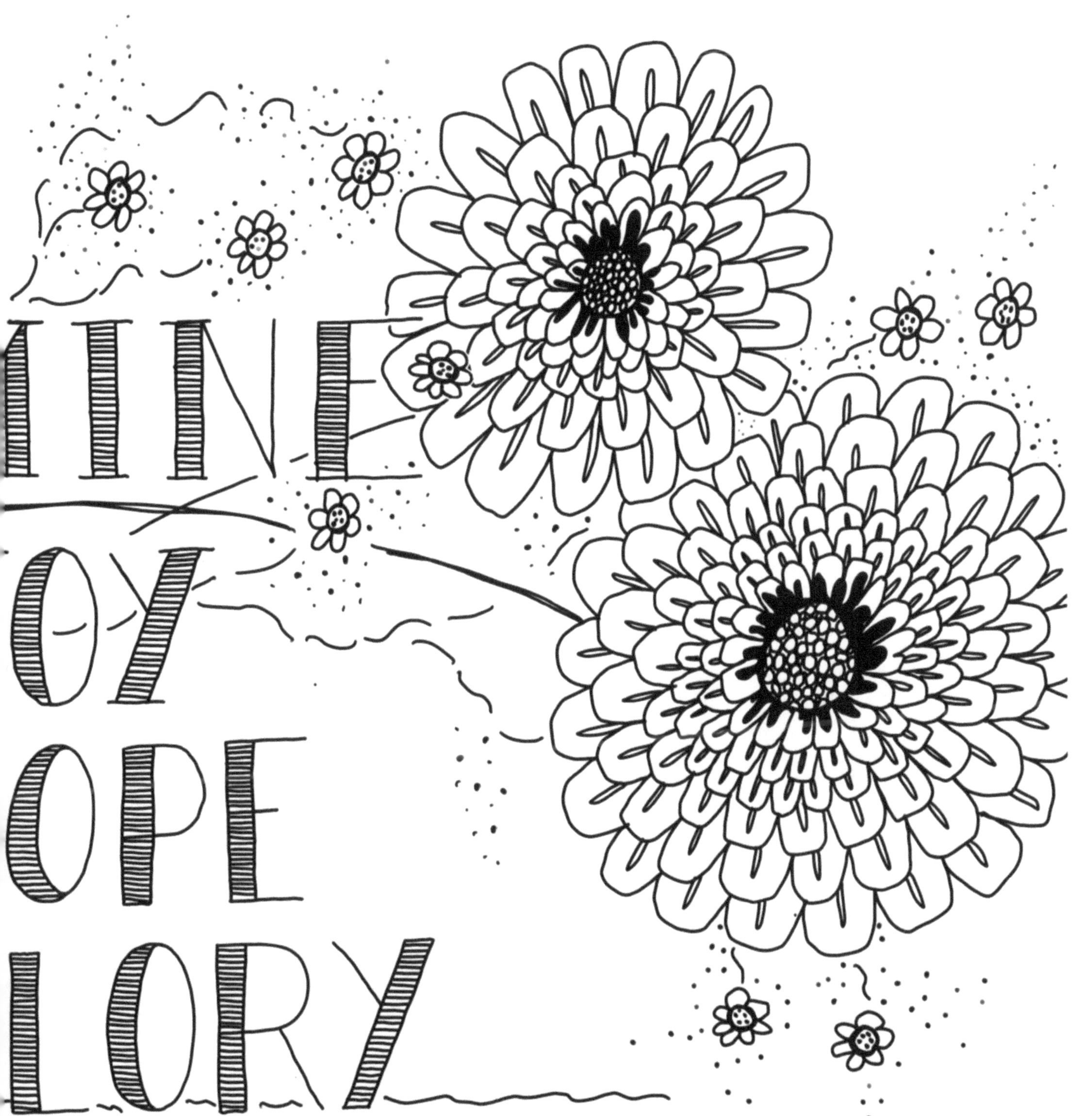
IINE
OY
OPE
LORY

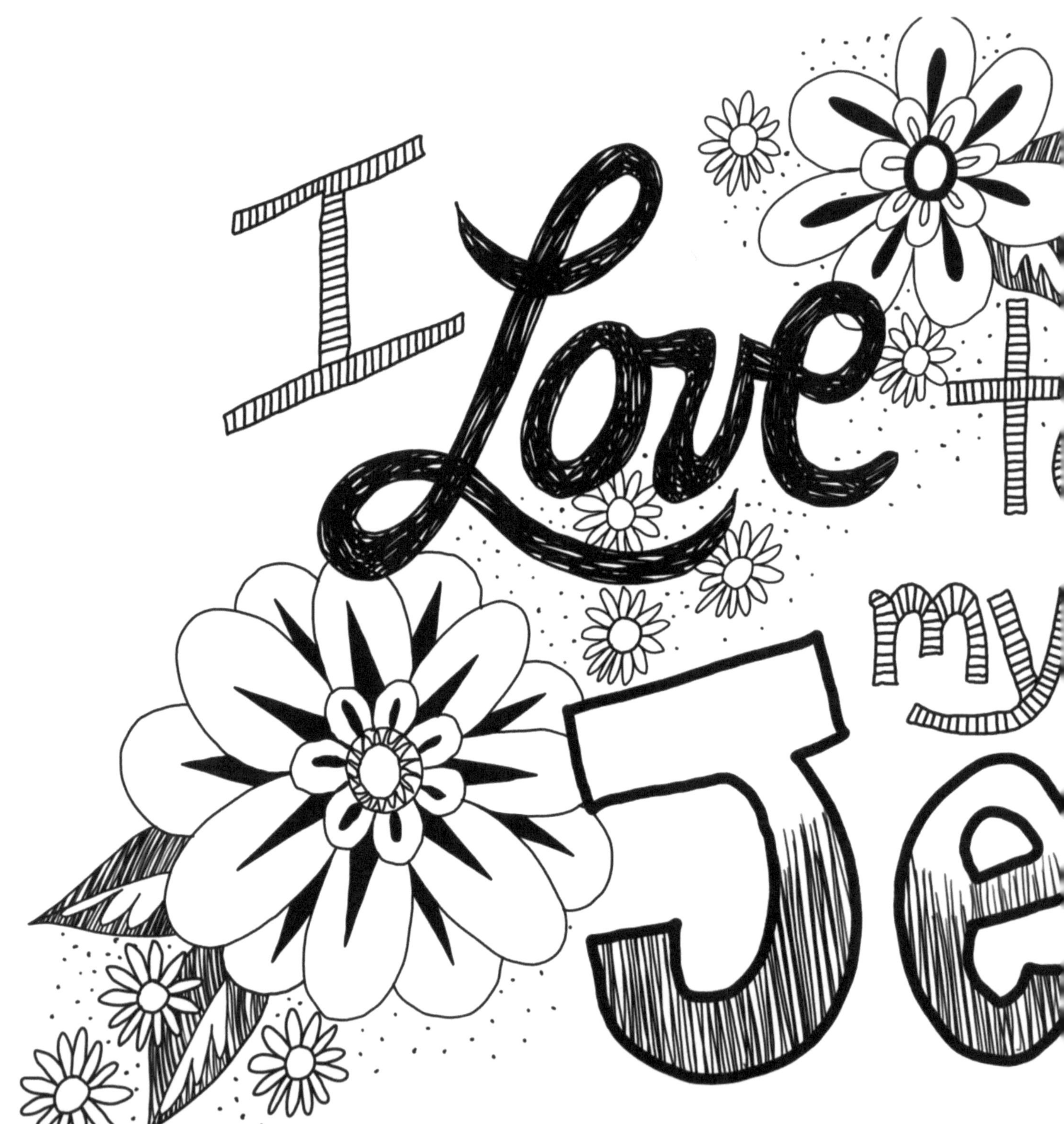

I Love to my Je

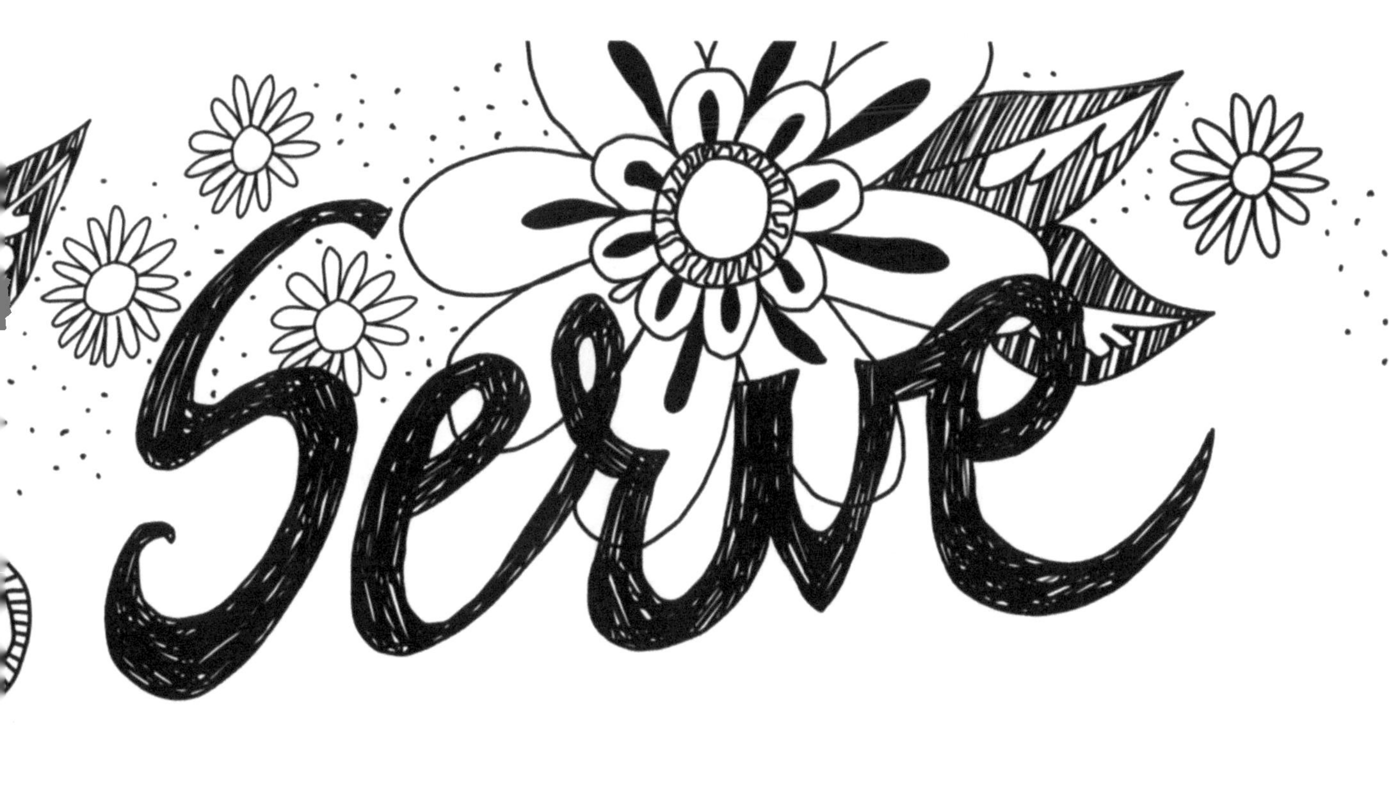

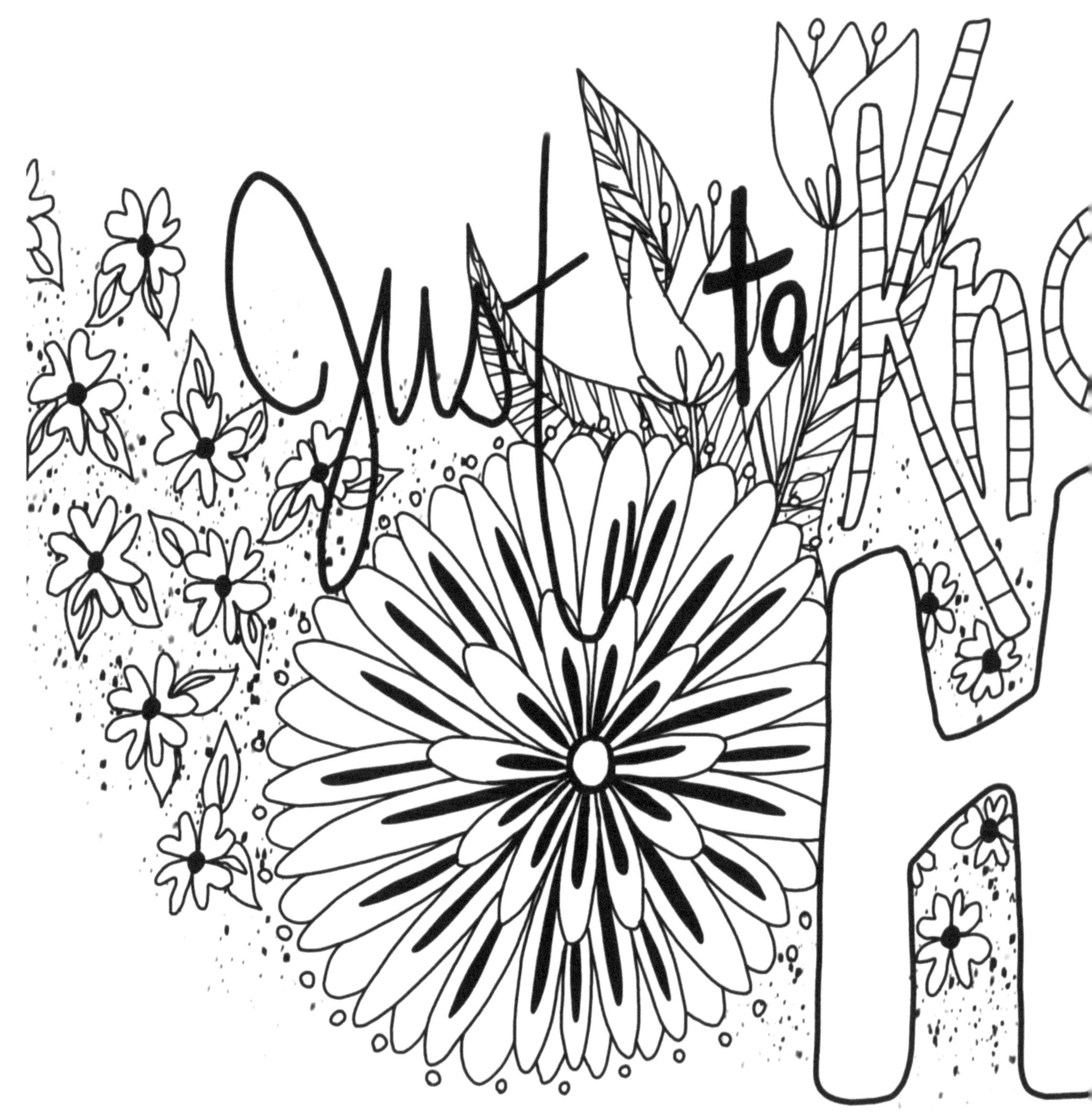
Just to Kno

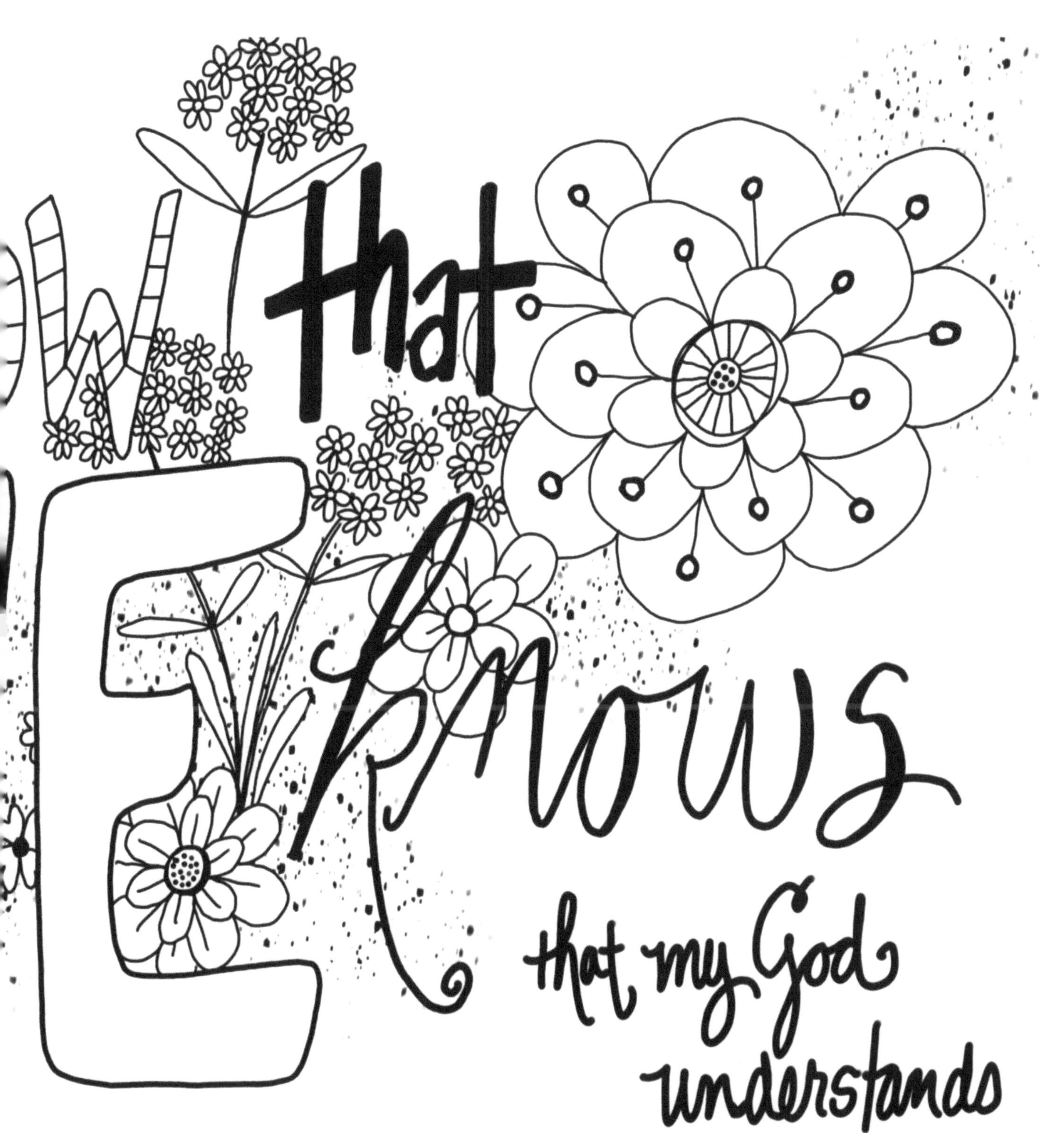
that
knows
that my God
understands

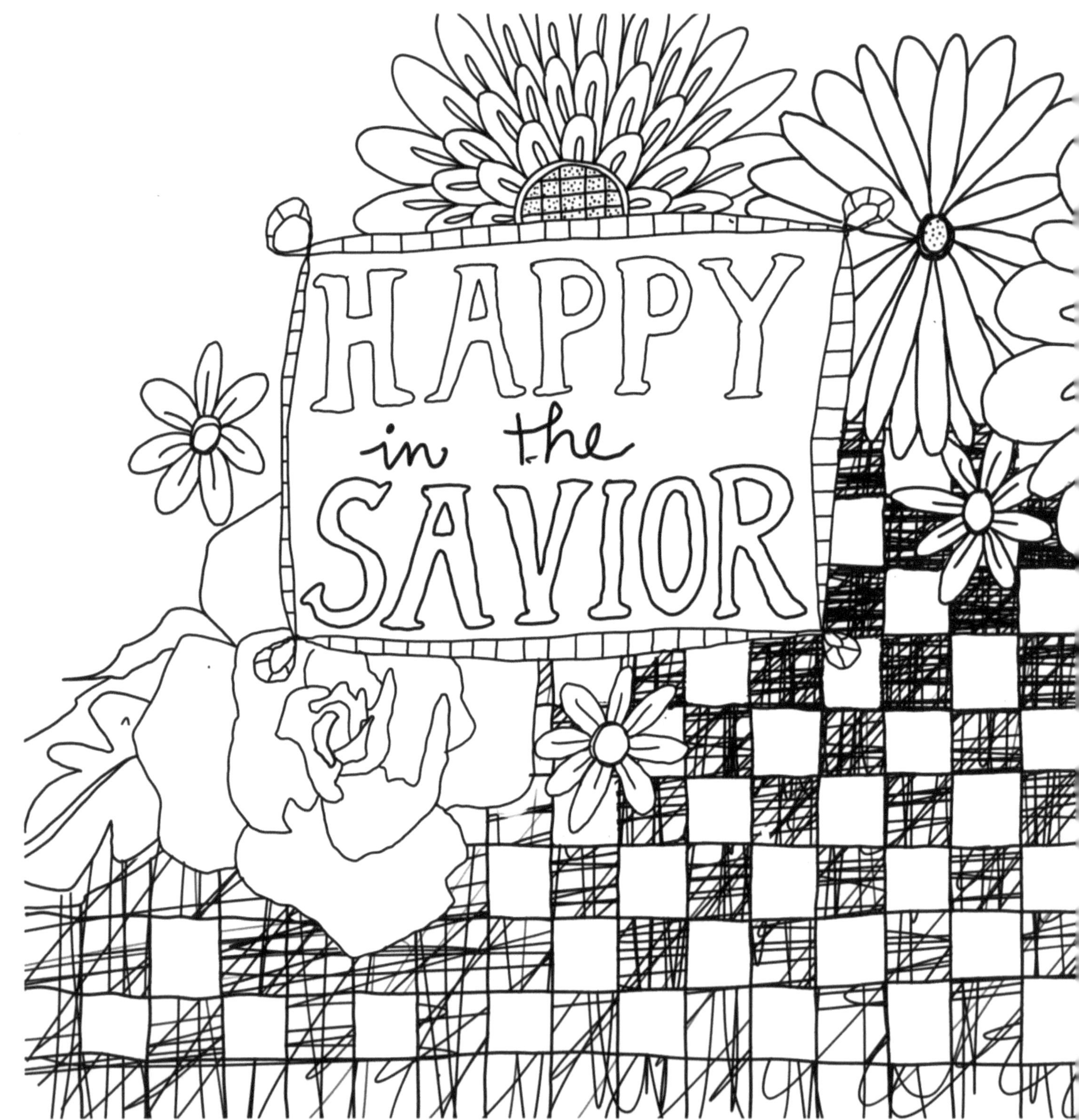

HAPPY
in the
SAVIOR

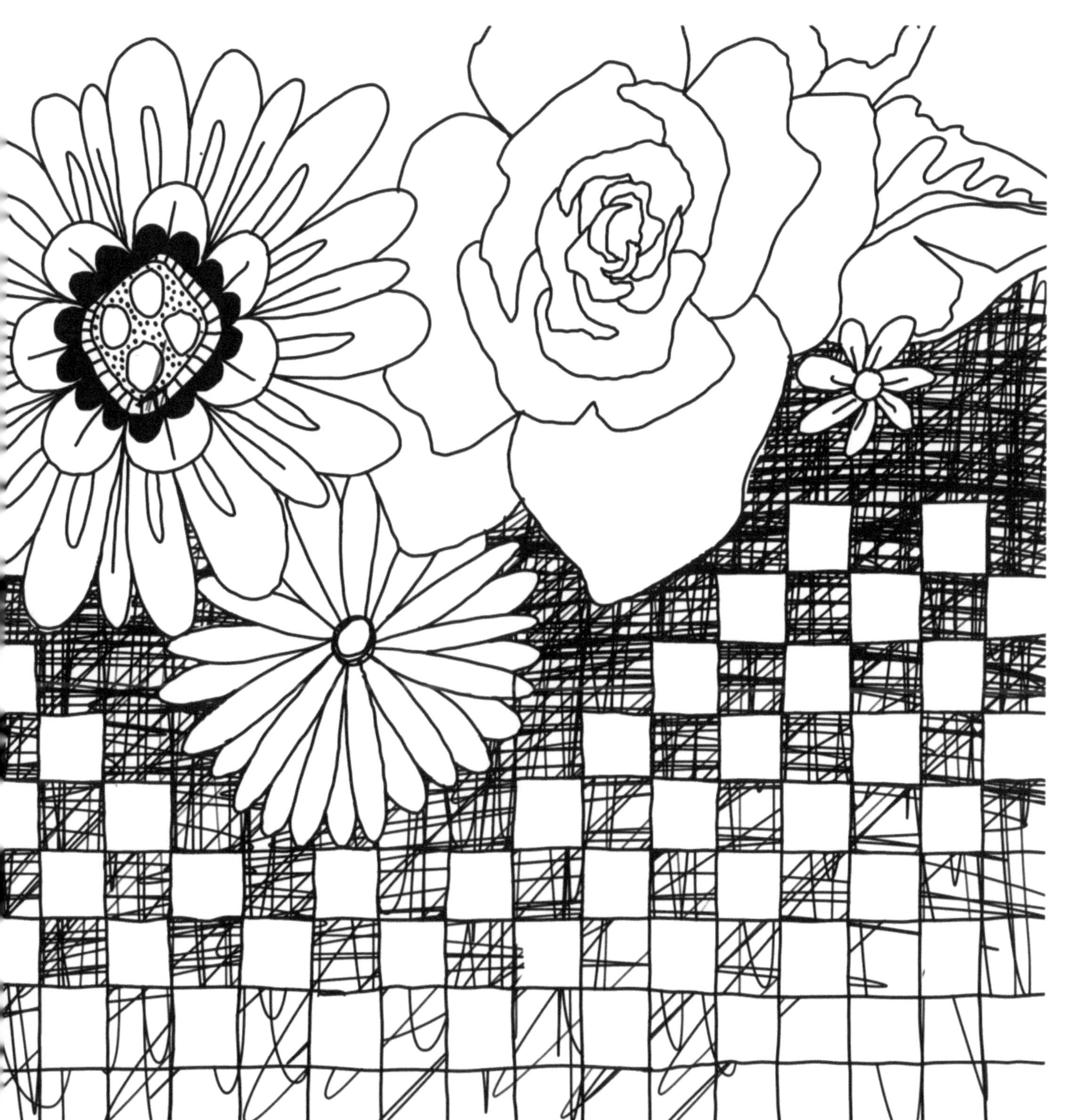

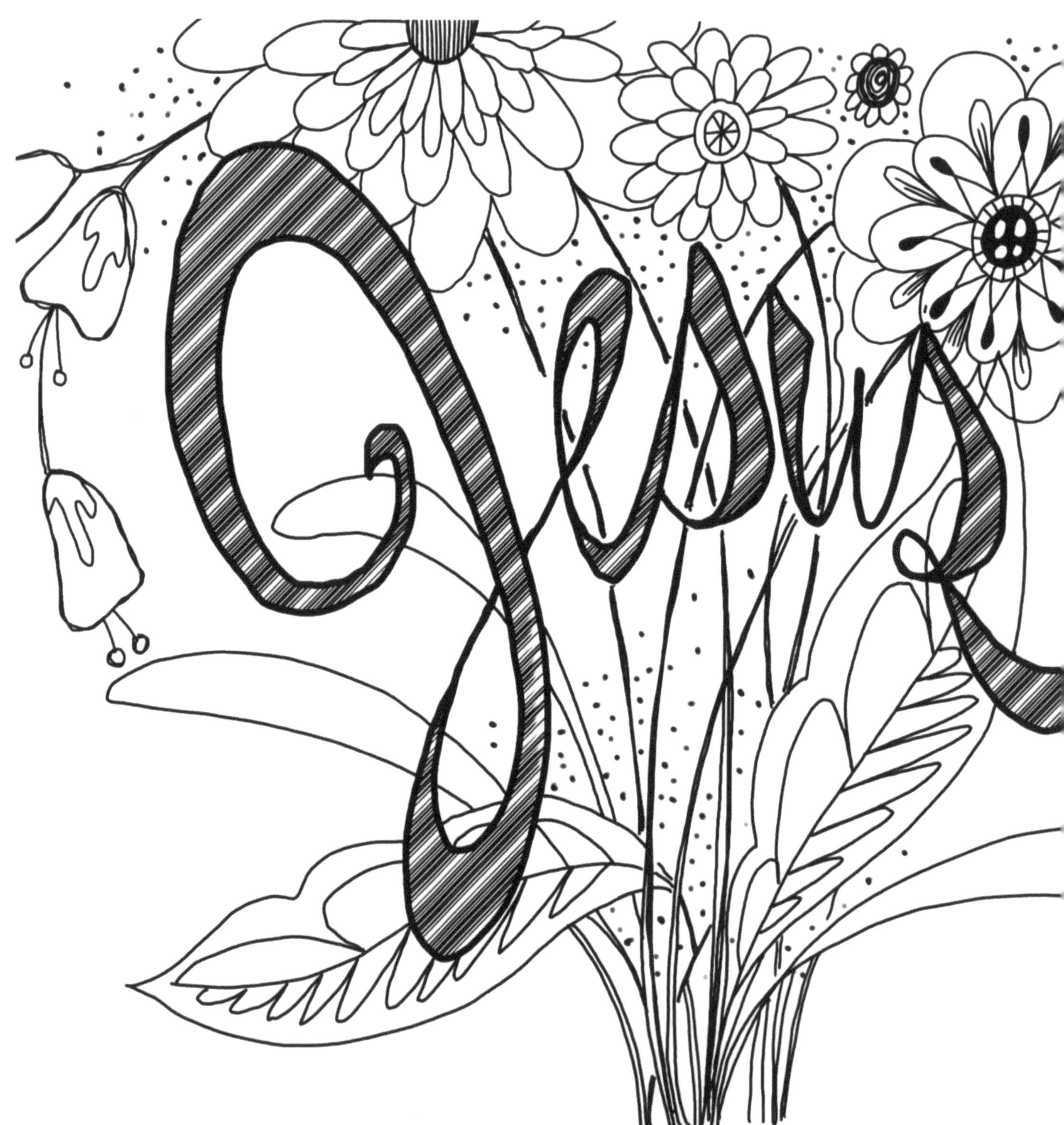
Jesus

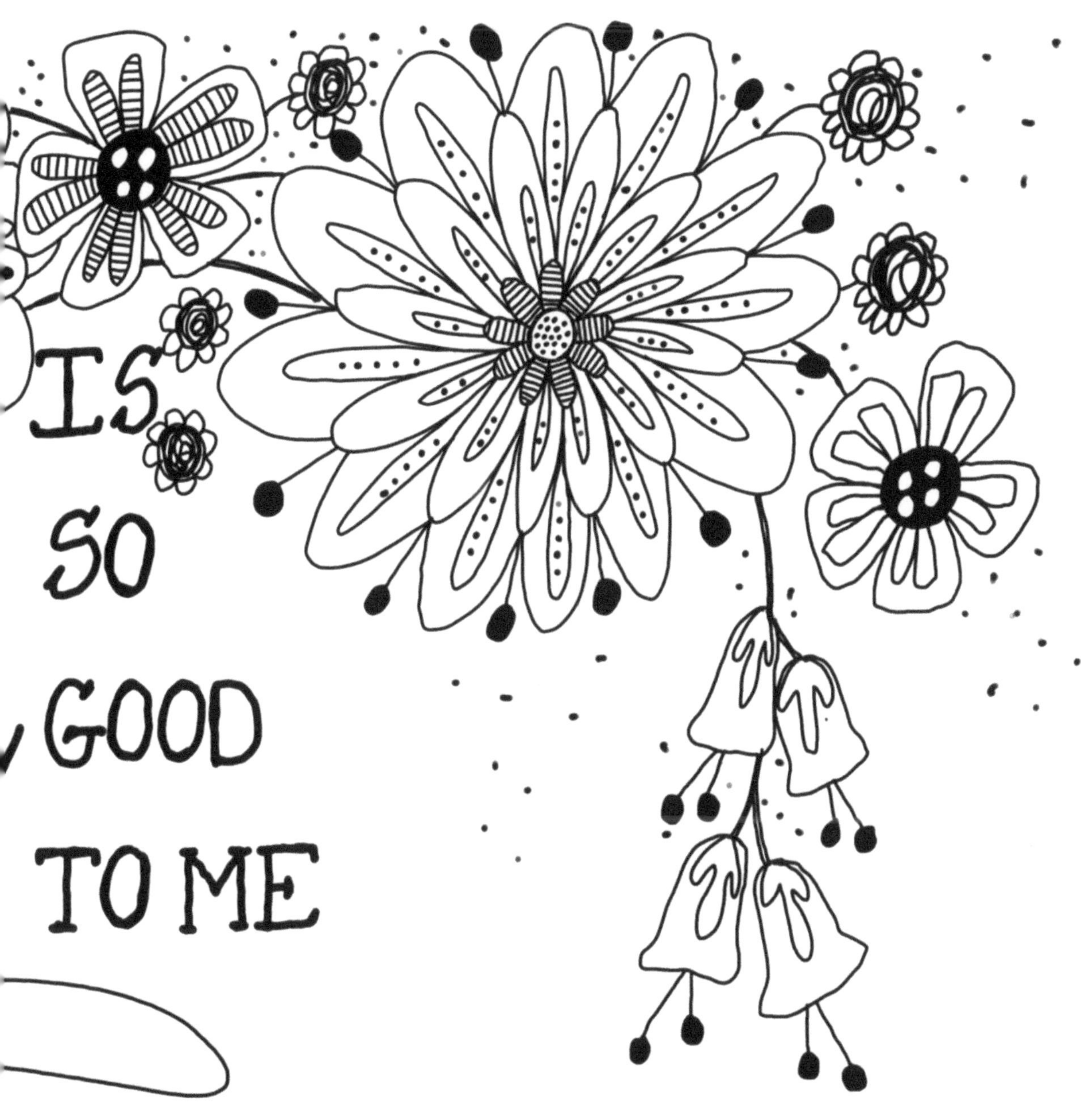

IS
SO
GOOD
TO ME

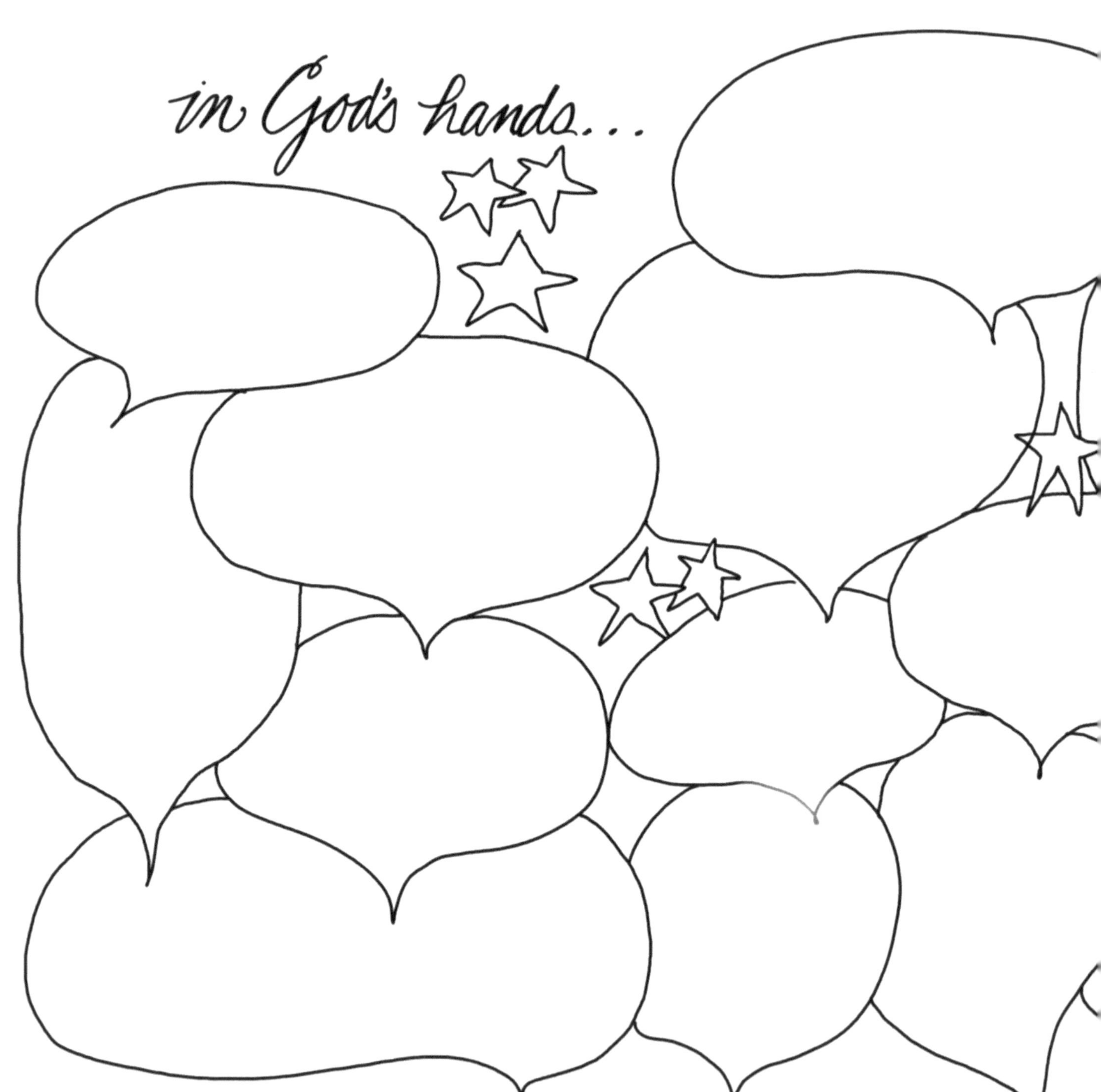
in God's hands....

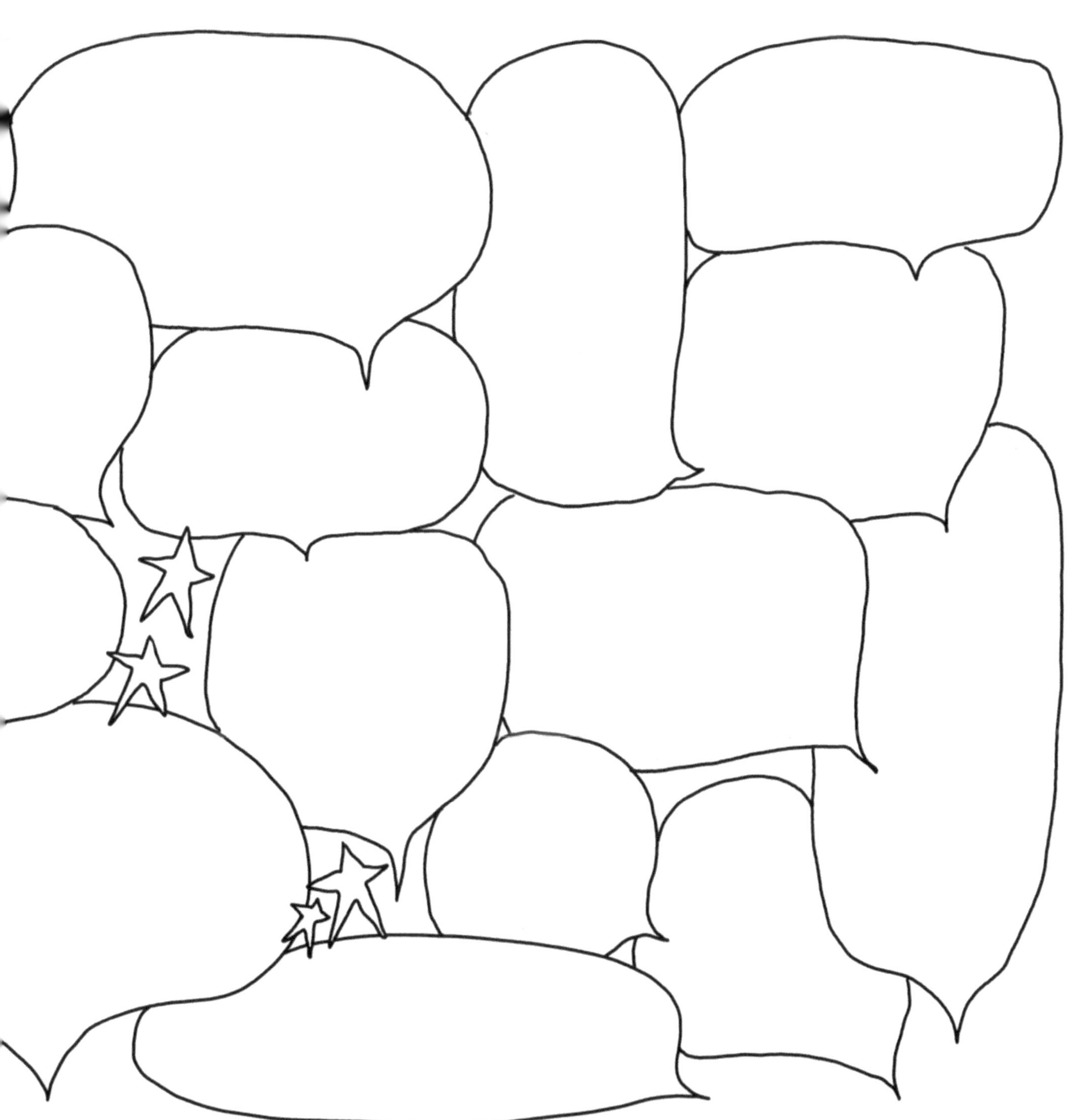

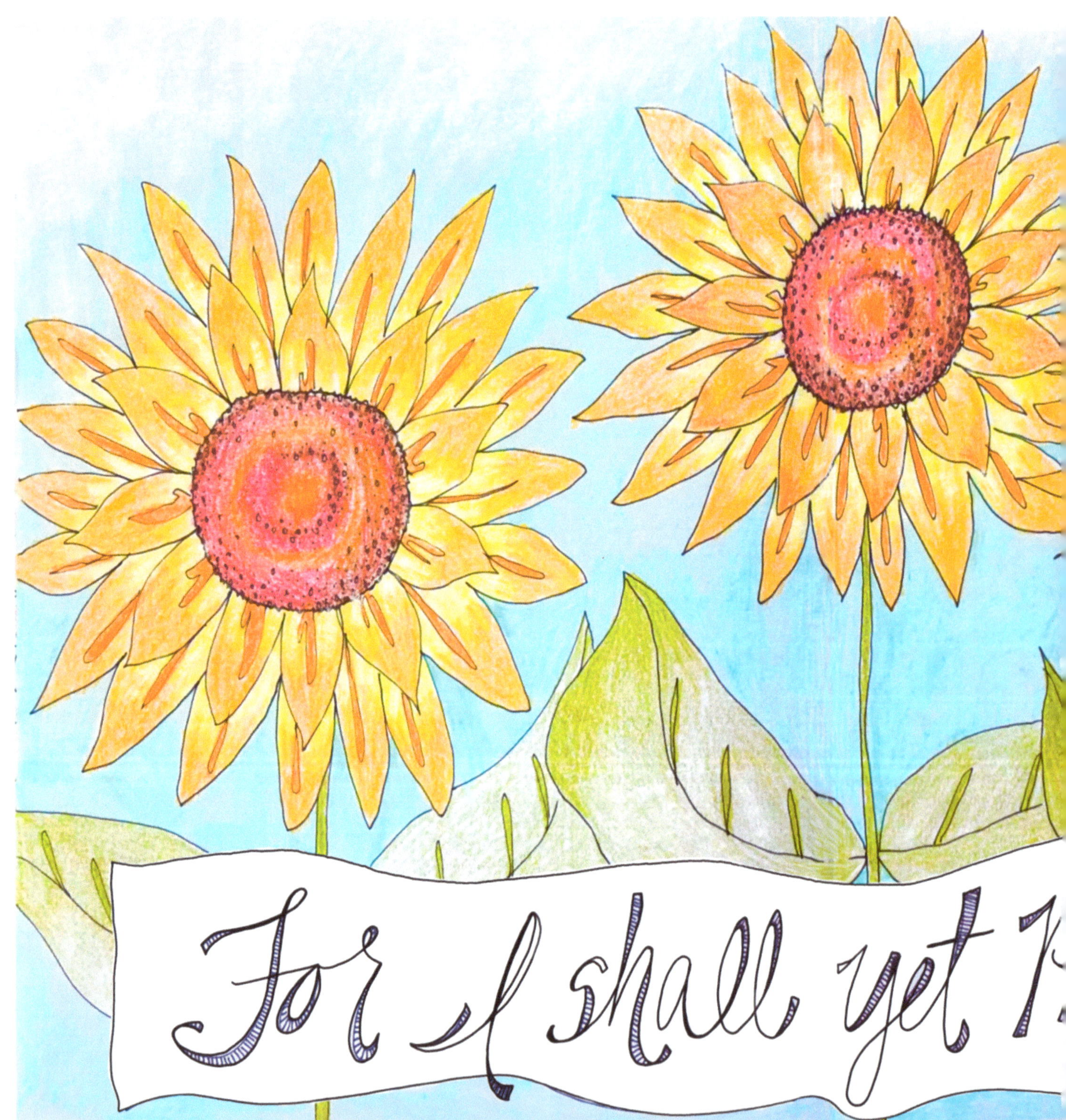

For I shall yet

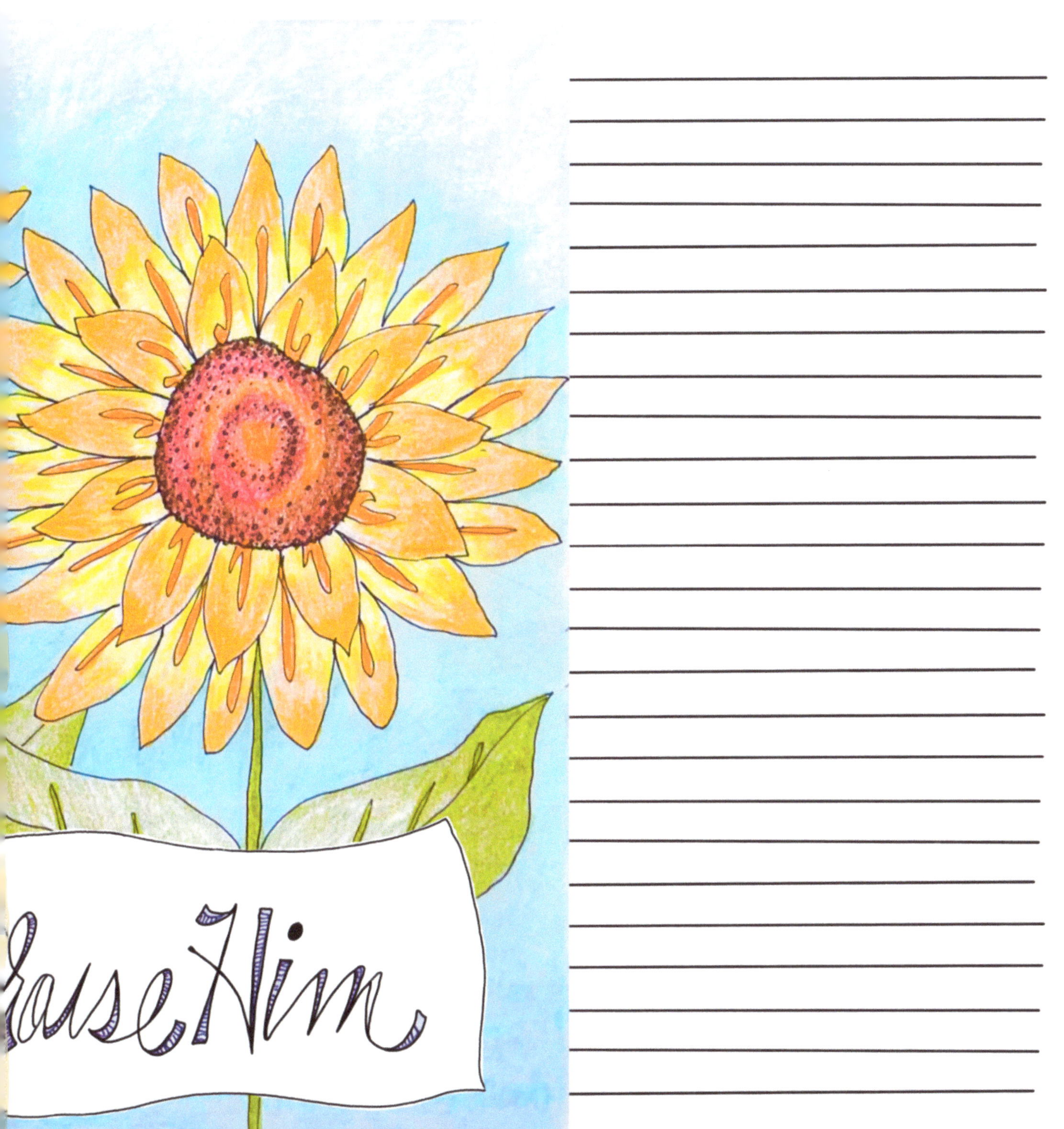
ause Him

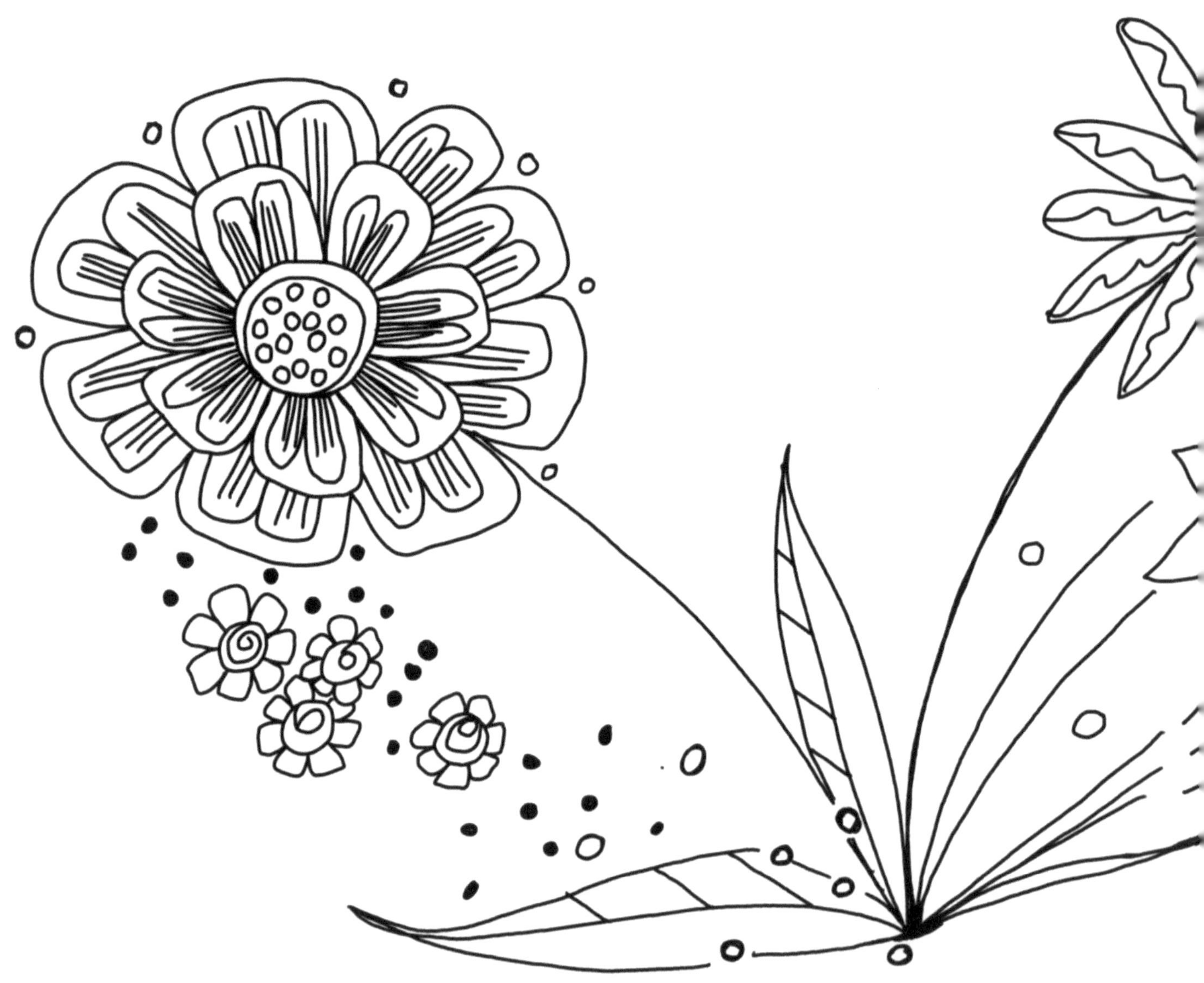

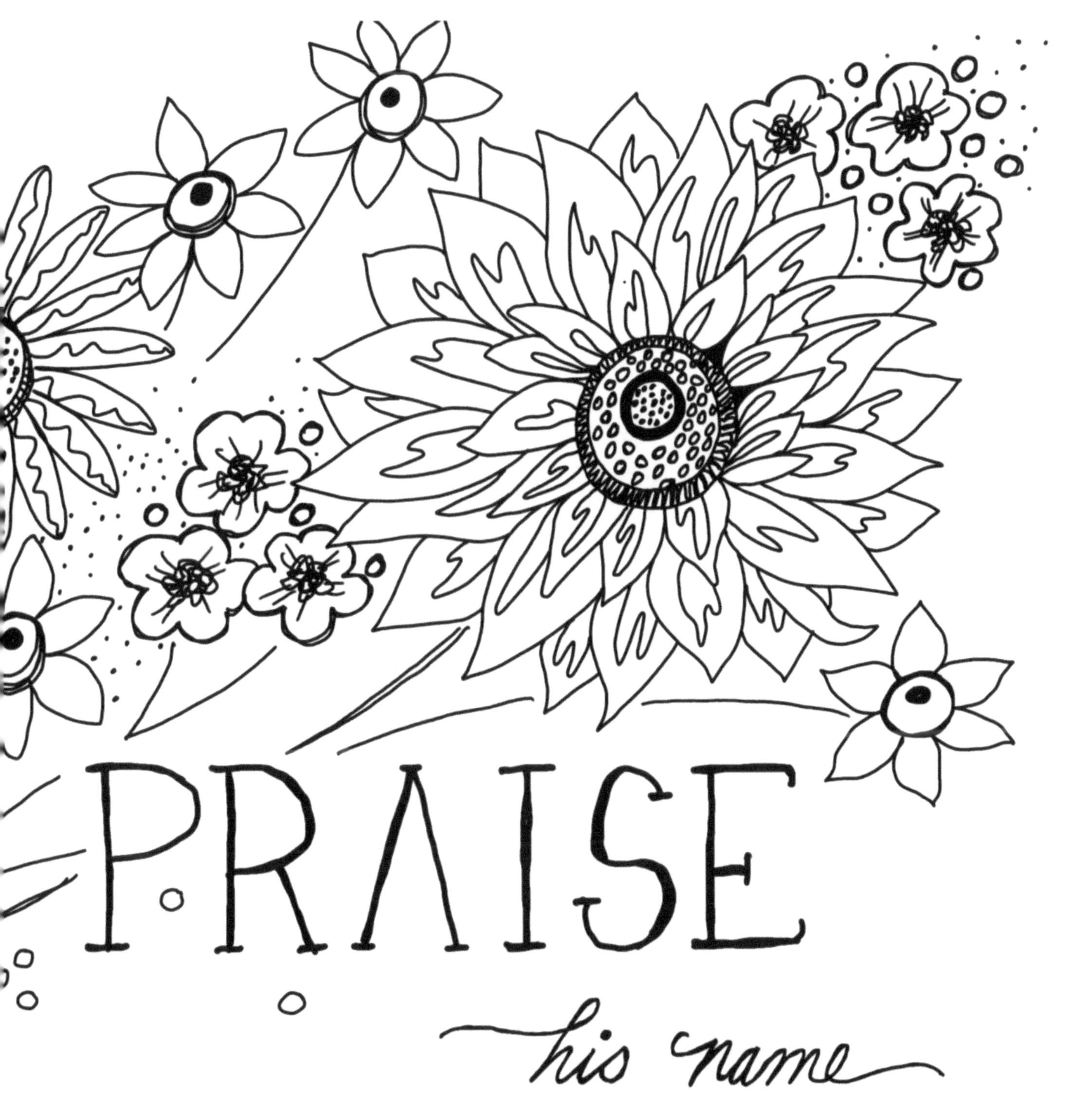

PRAISE
his name

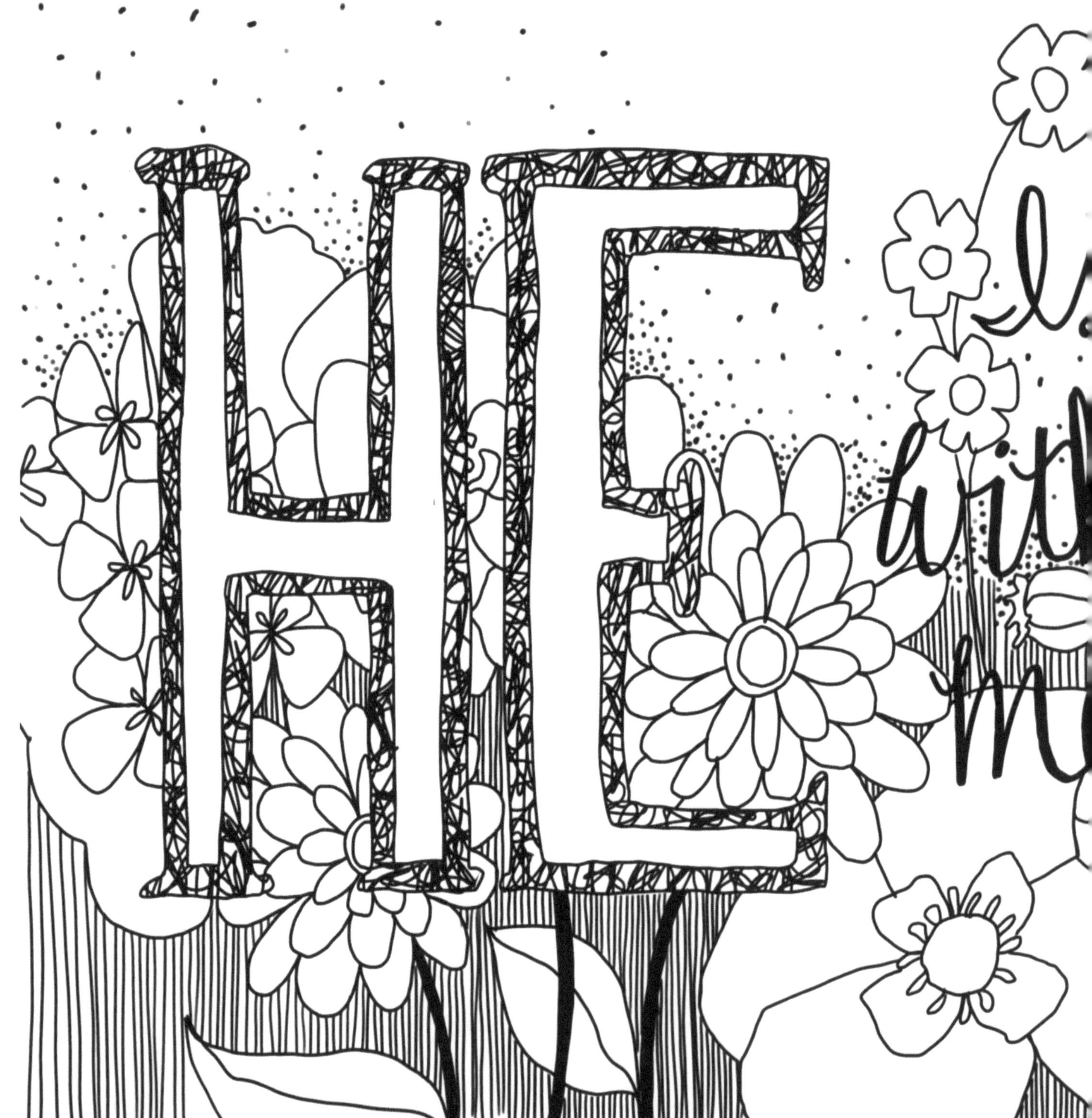

HE
is with
me

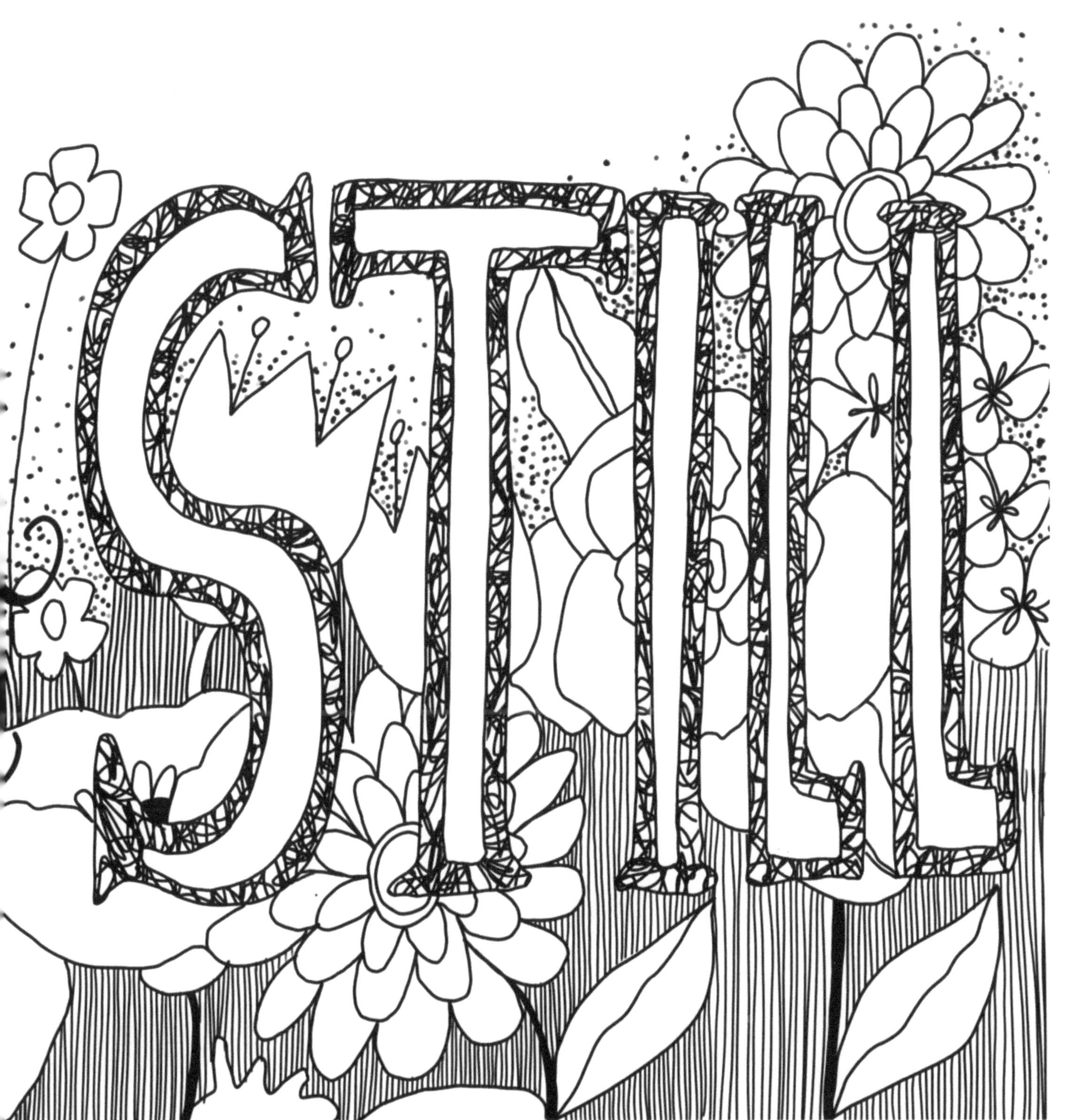

STILL

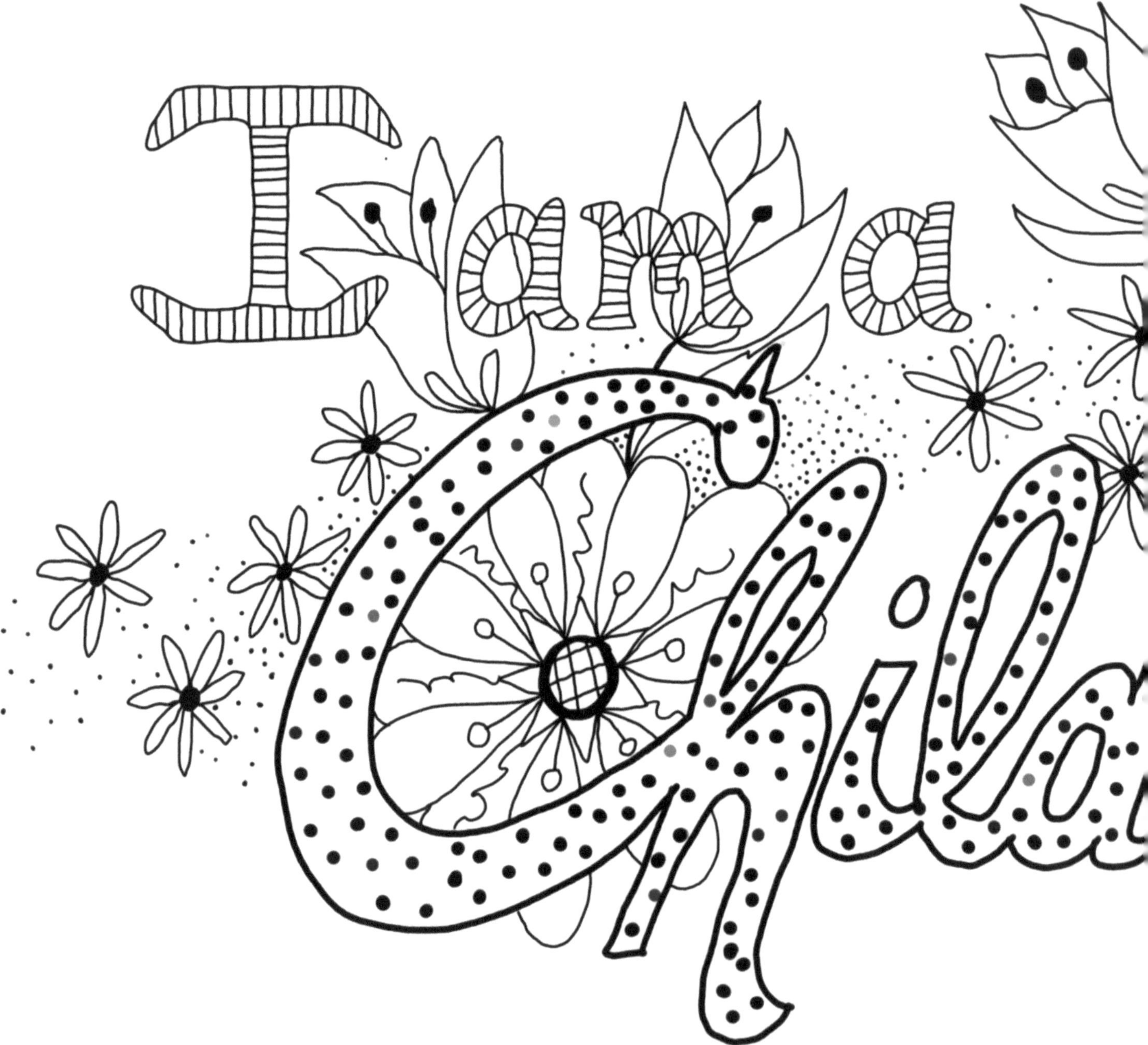

I am a
Child

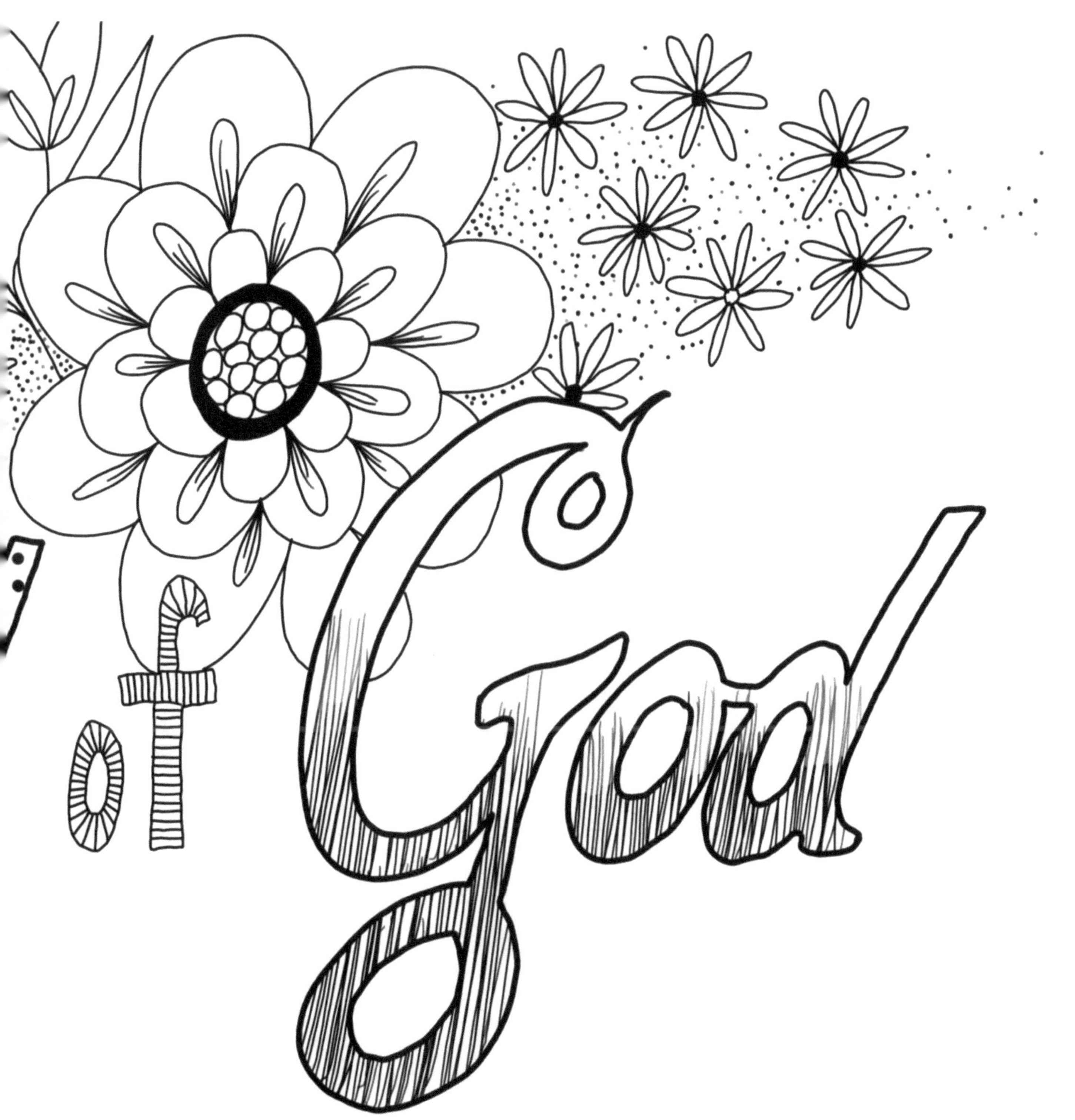

God

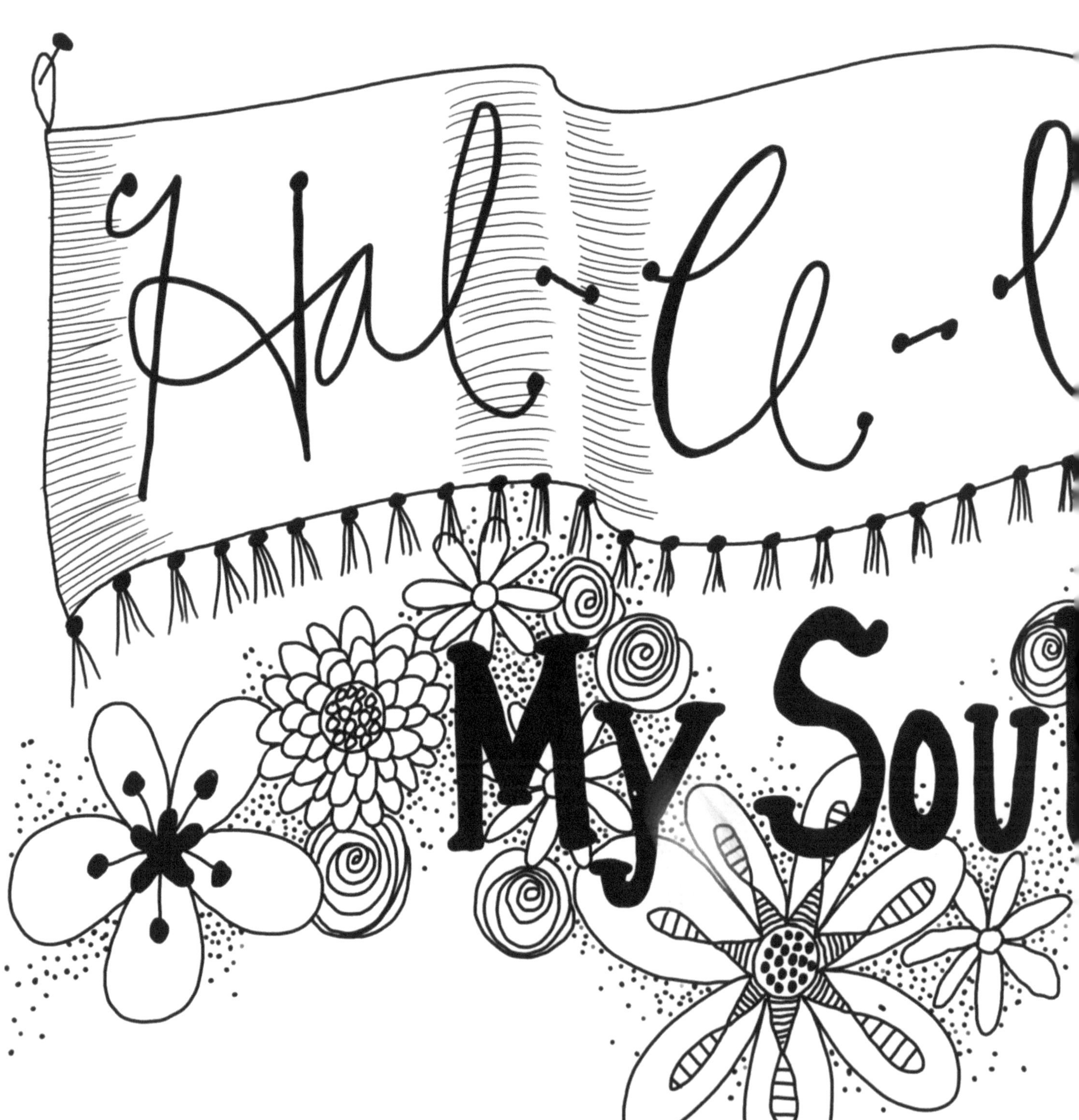

Hal-le-lu
My Soul

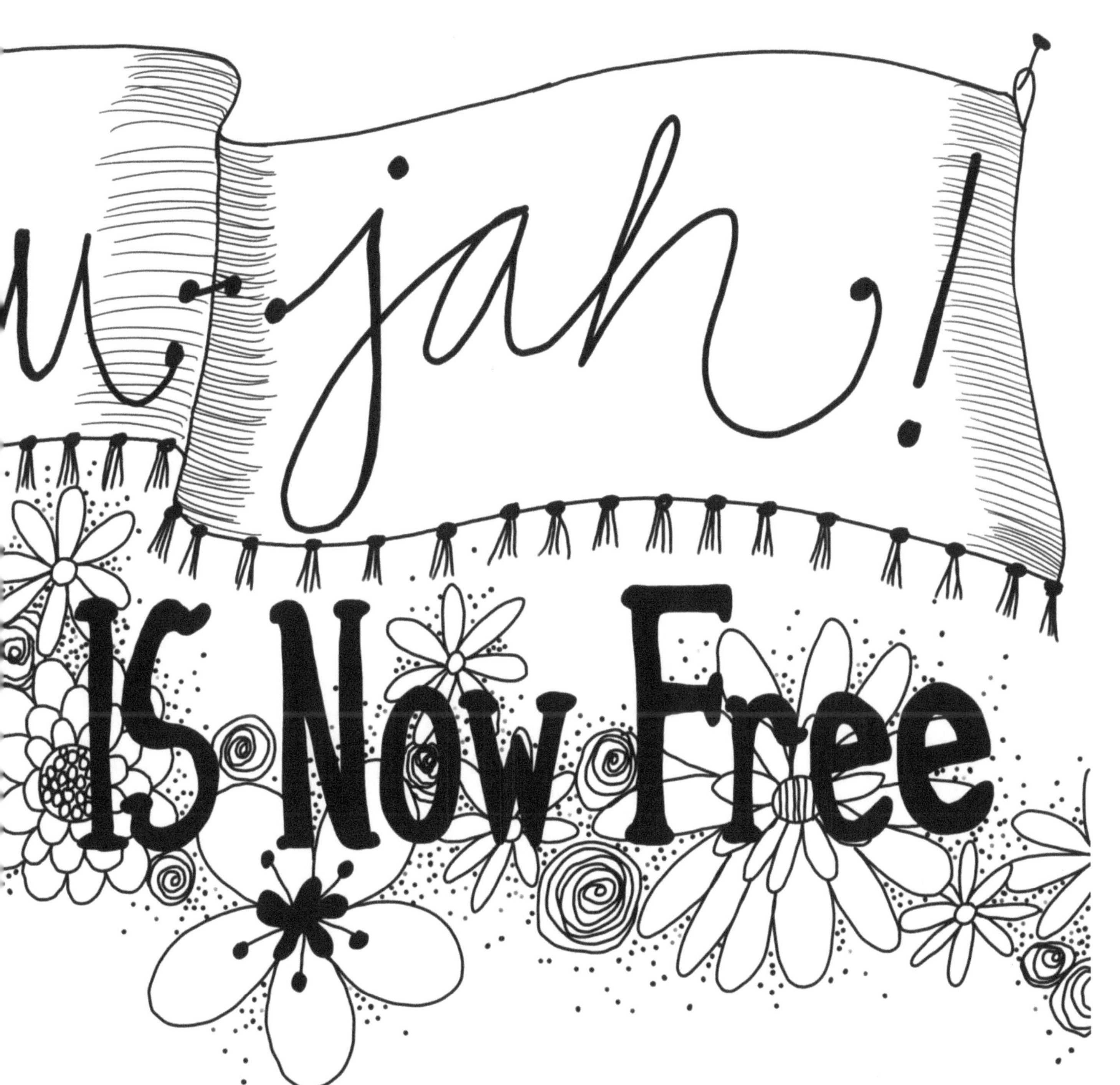
jah!
is Now Free

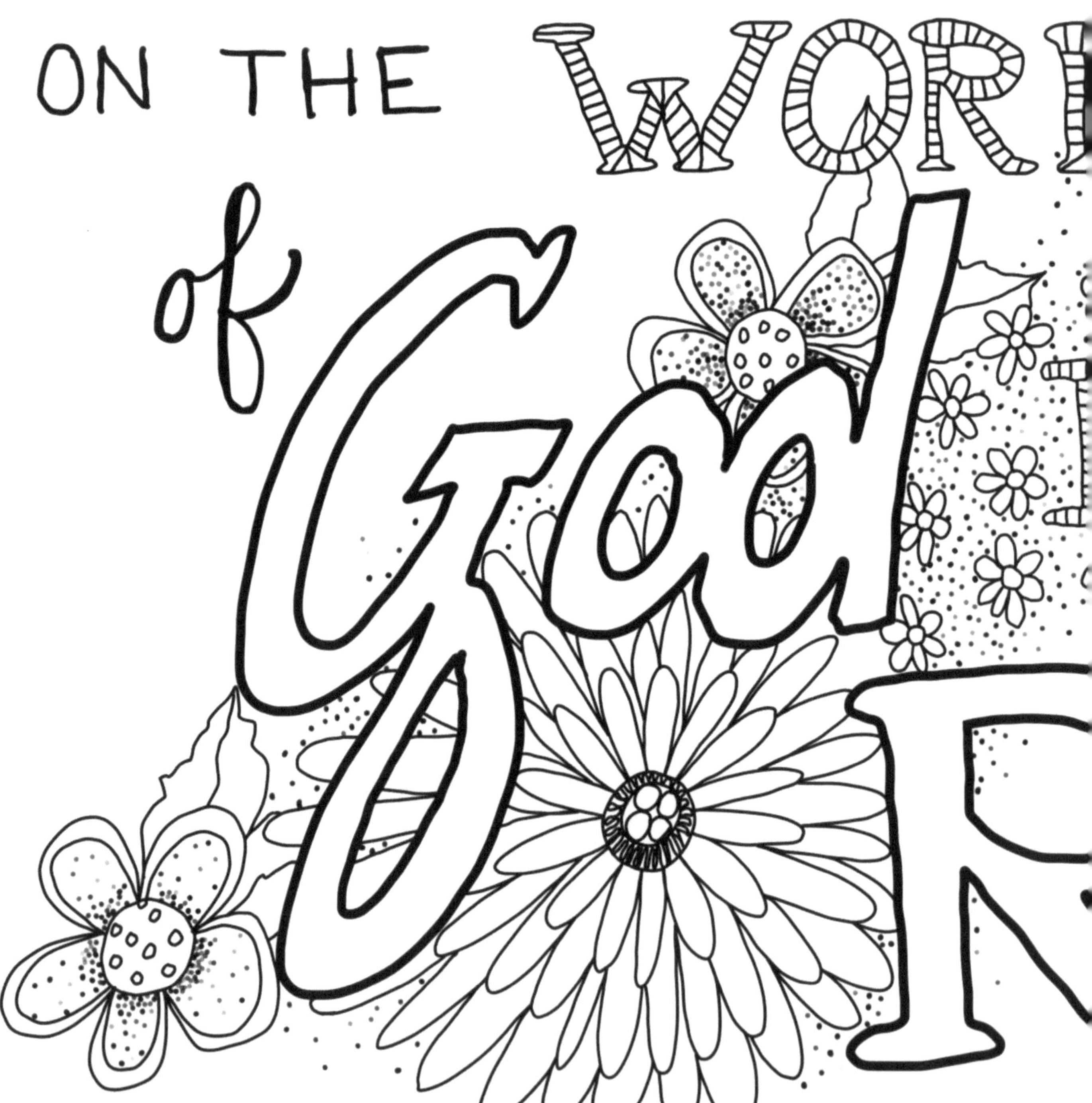

ON THE
WOR
of
God
OR

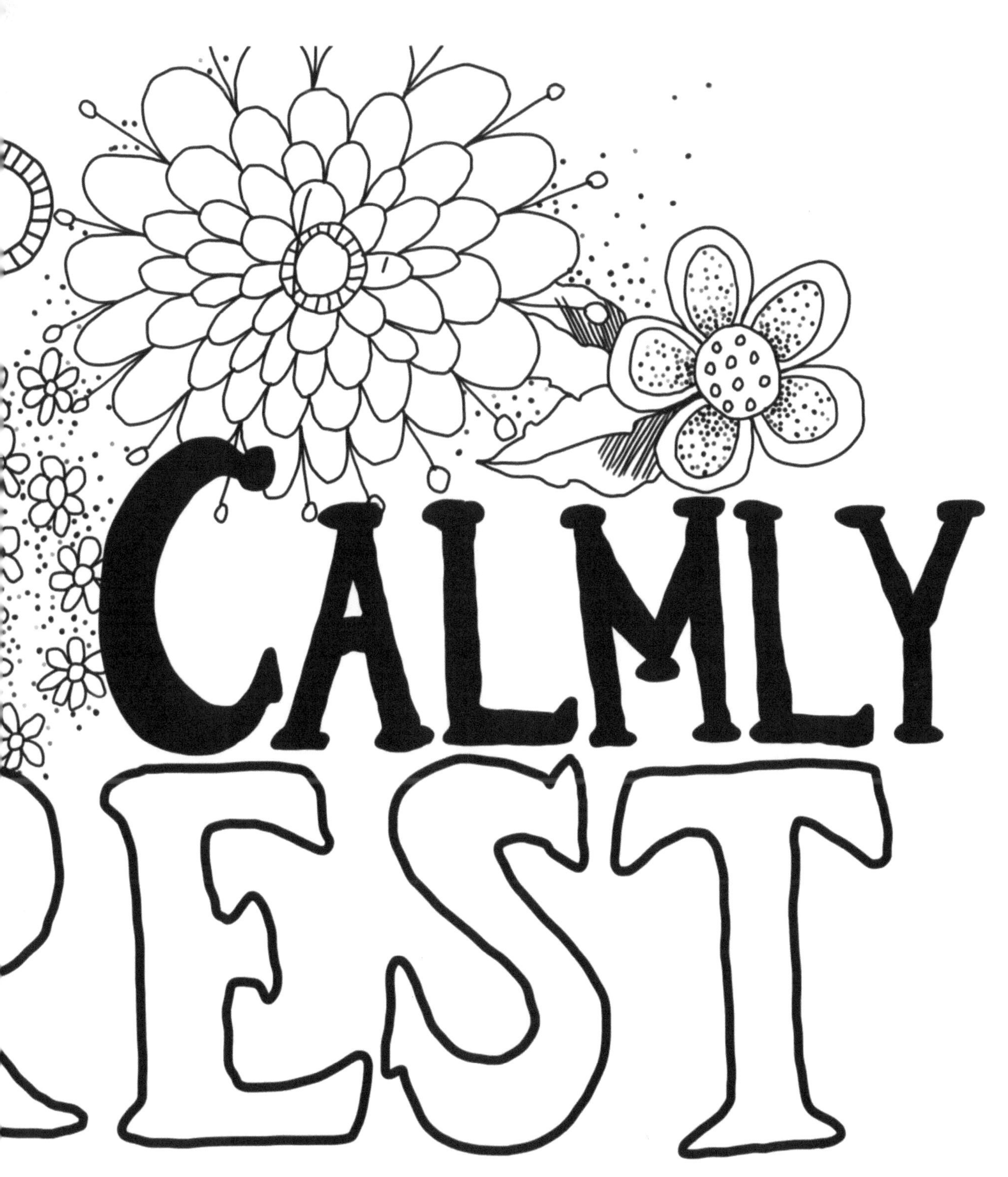
CALMLY
REST

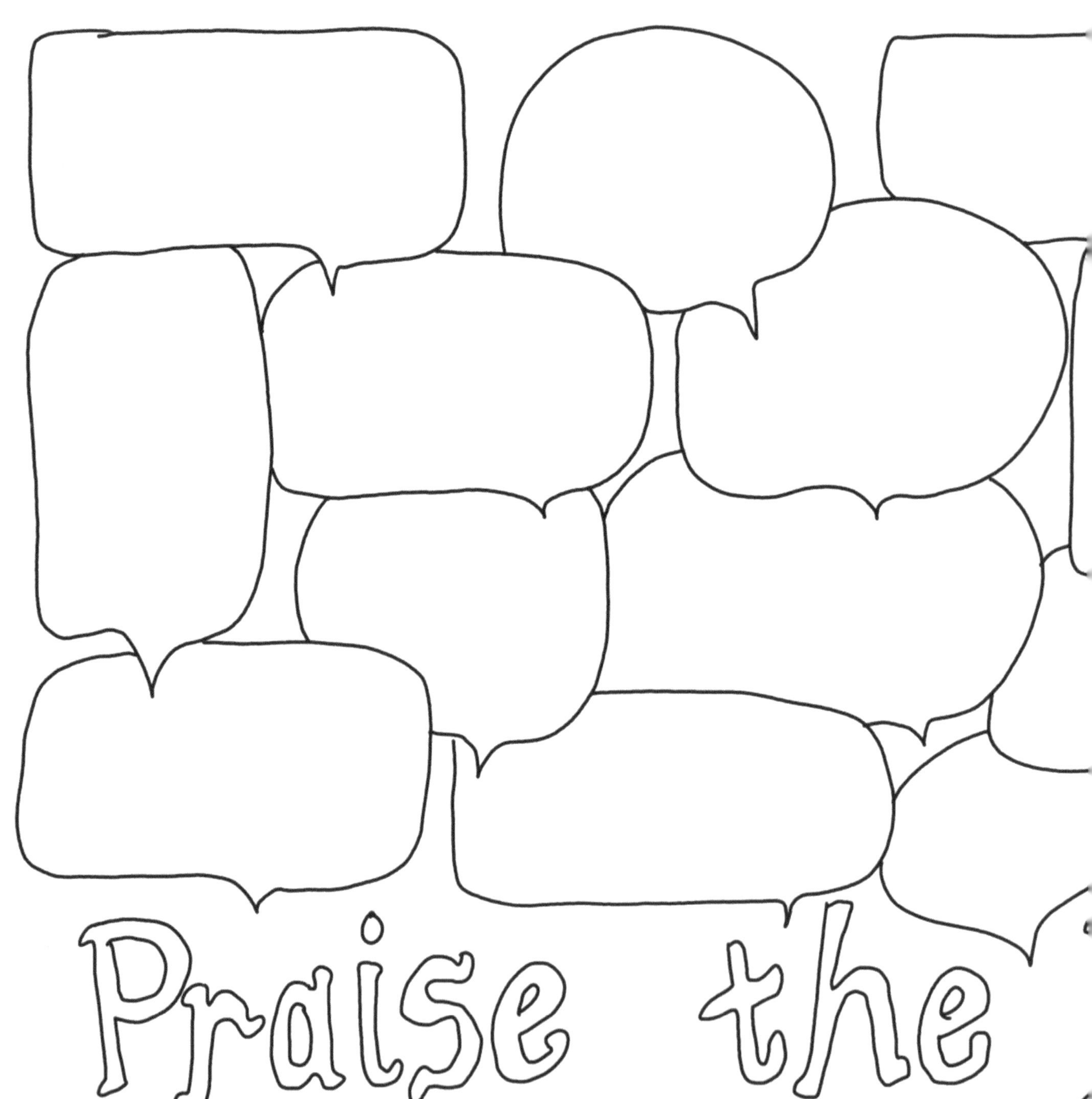
Praise the

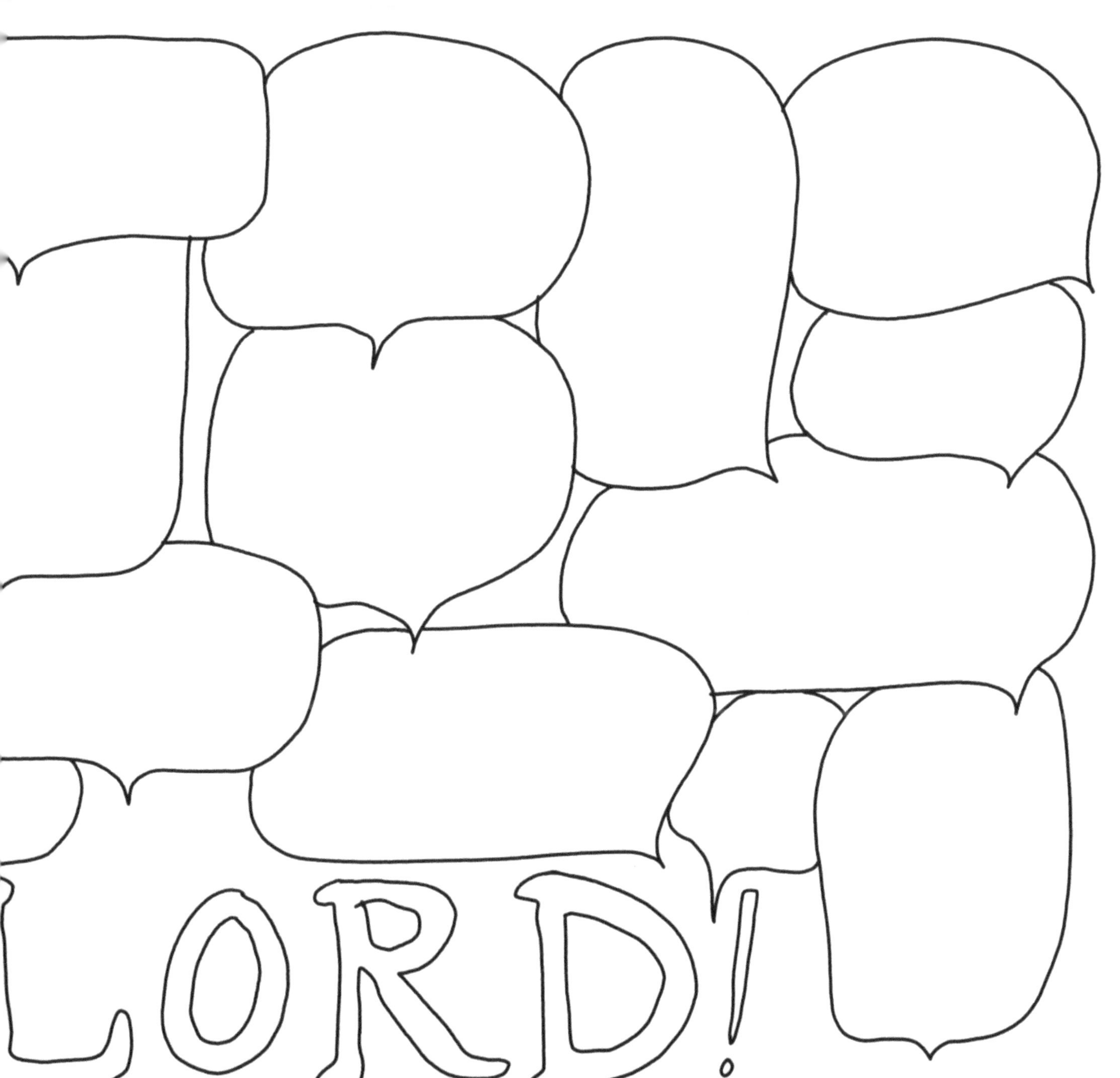

LORD!

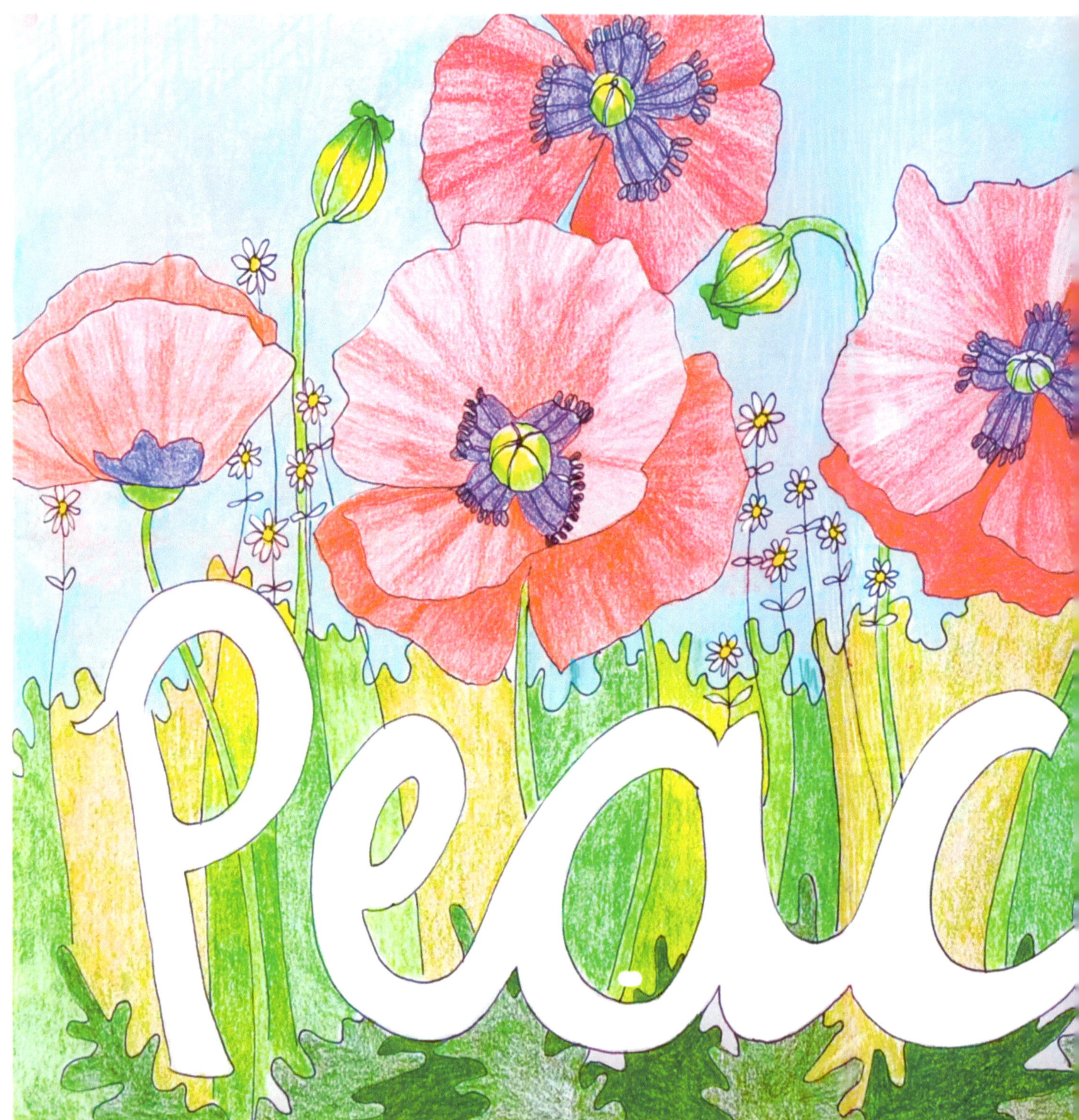

Pea

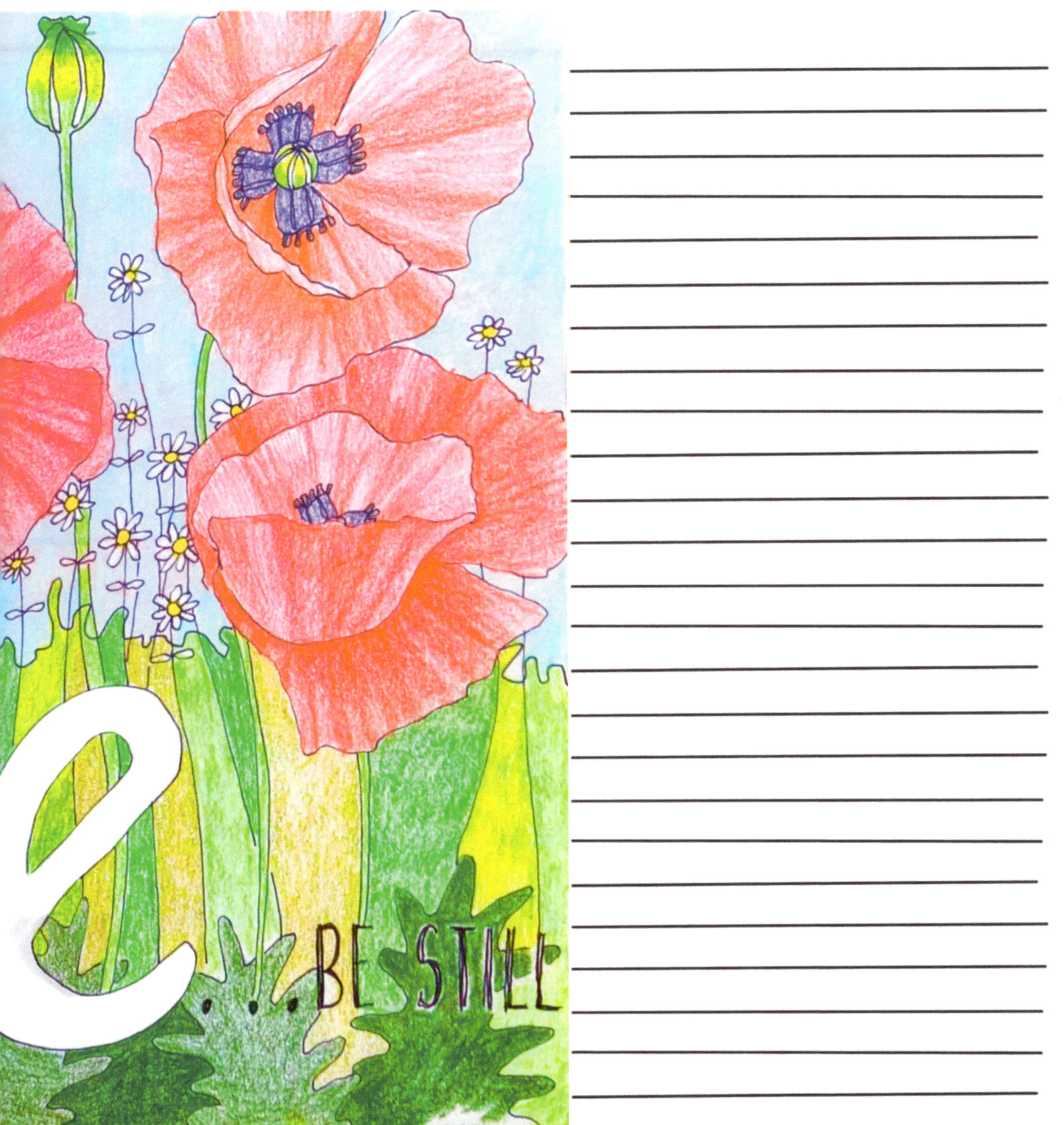
...BE STILL

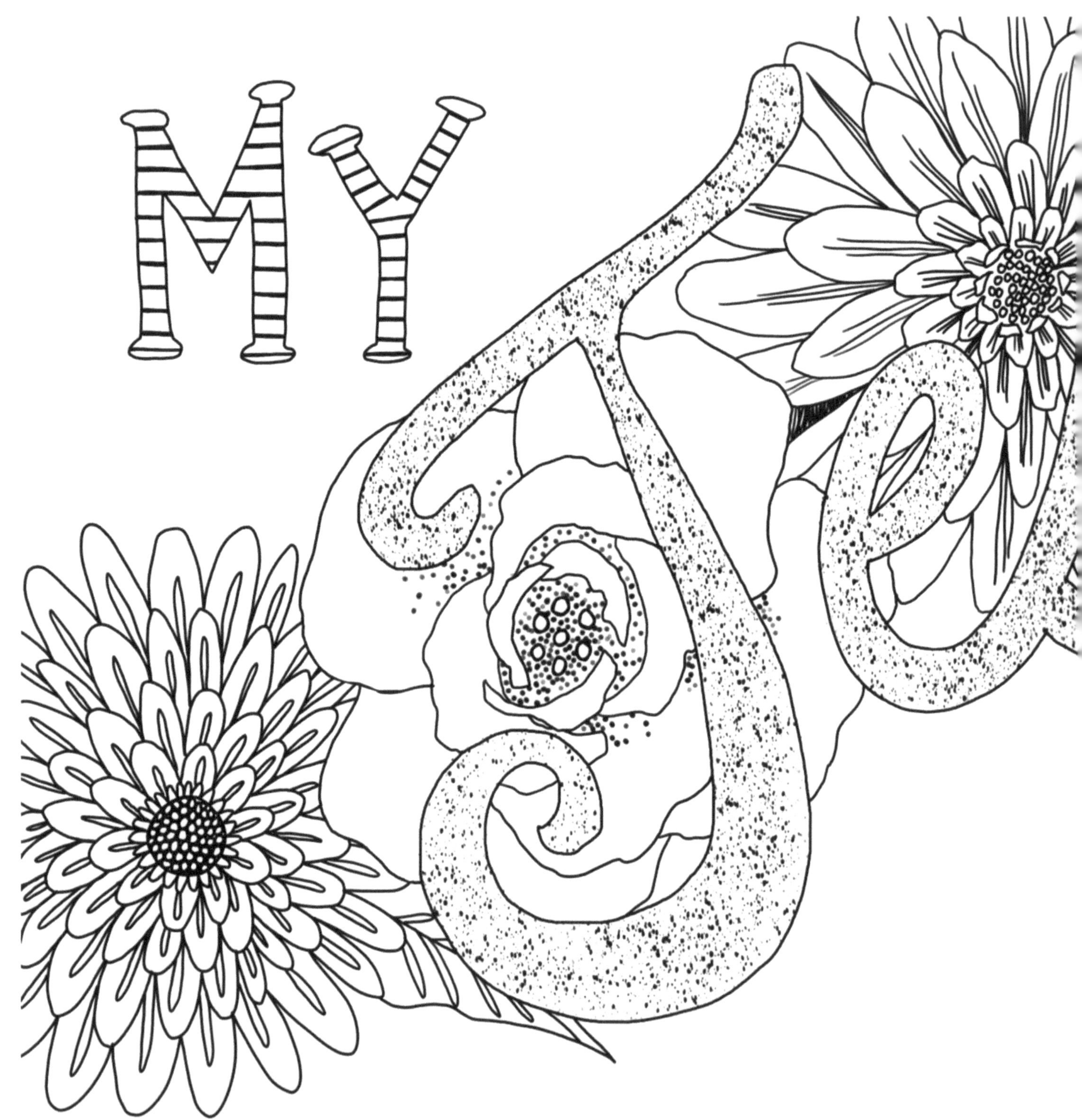
MY

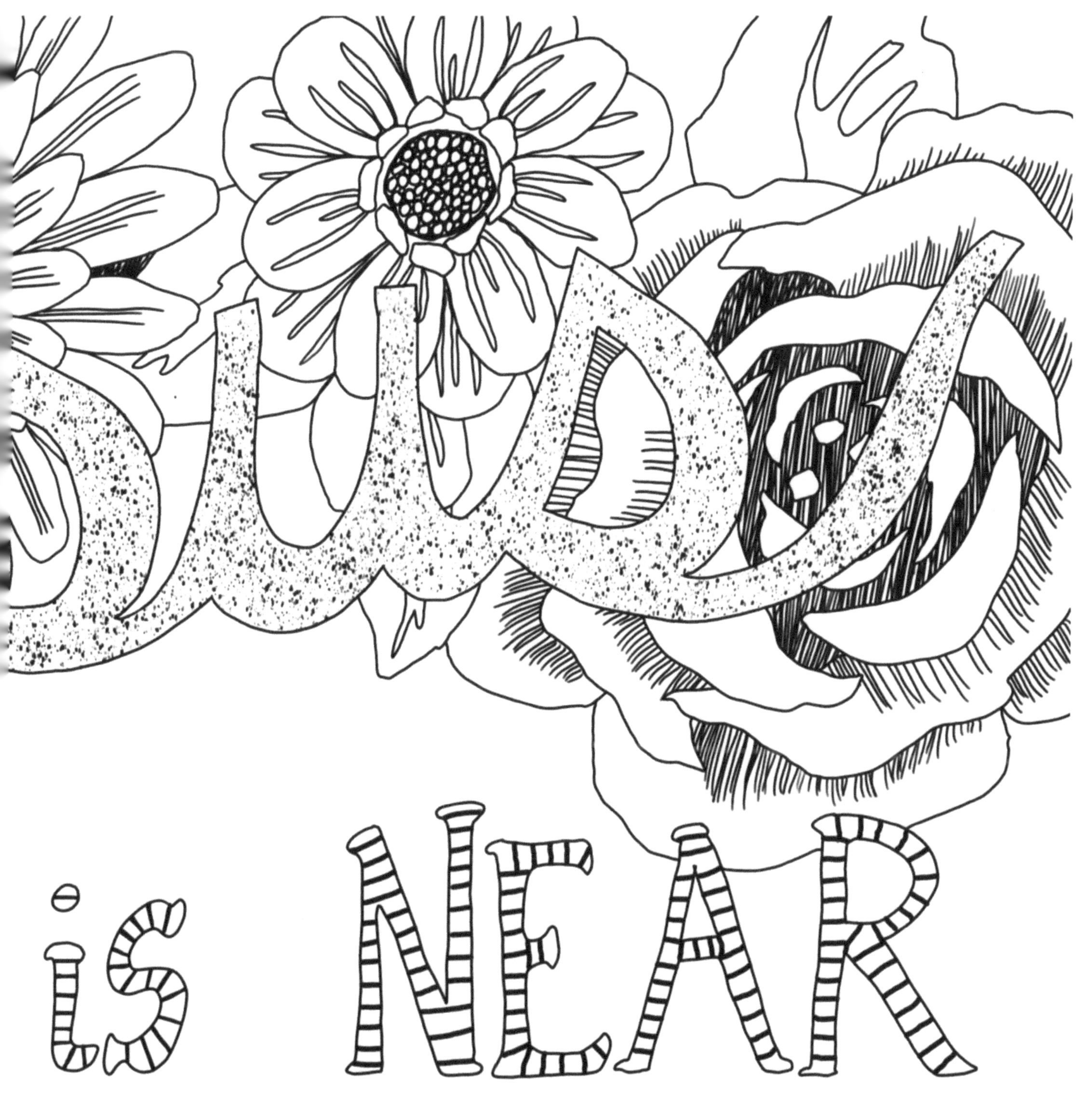

BUDS
is NEAR

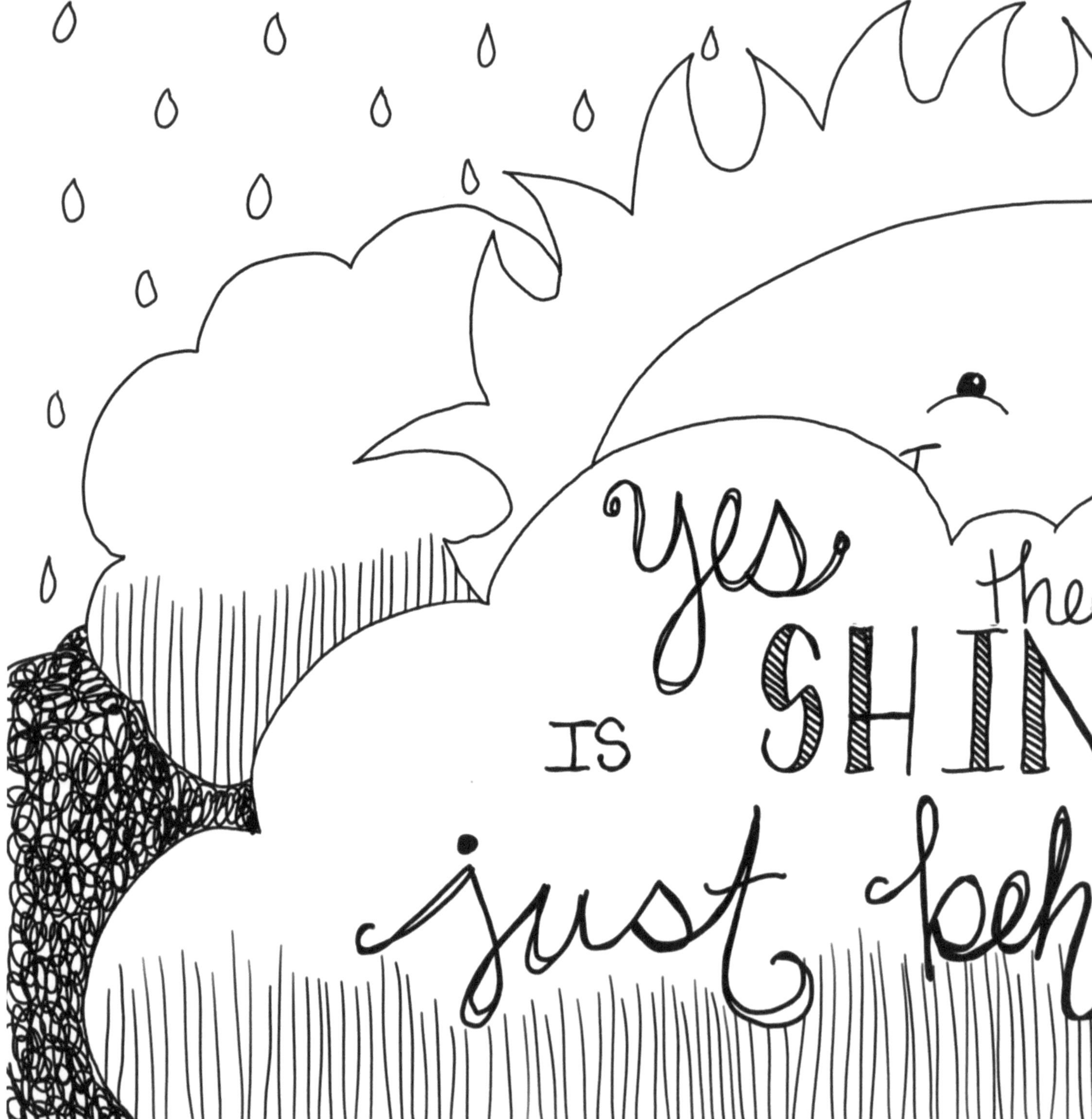

yes the
is SHIN
just beh

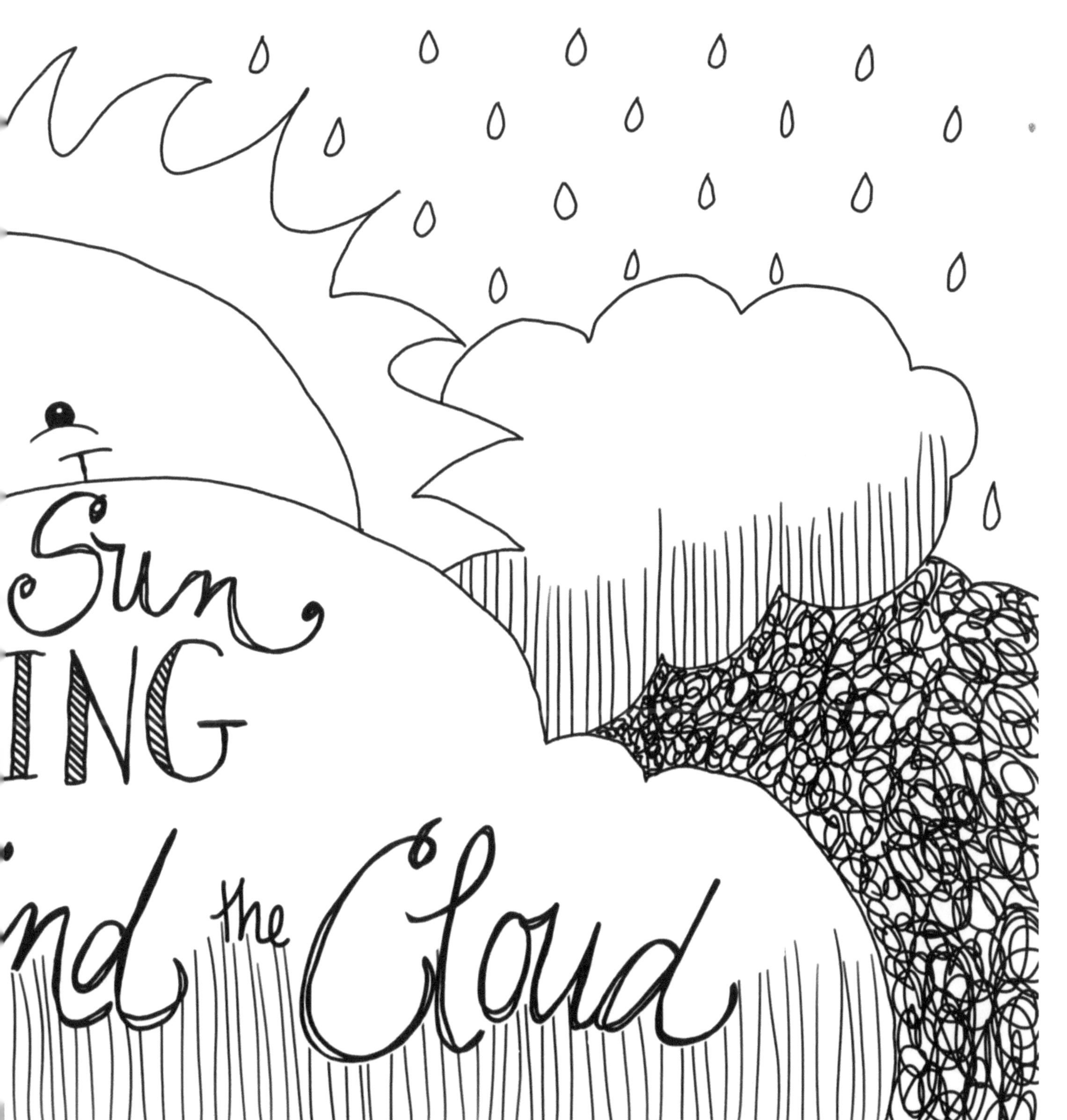
Sun
ING
nd the Cloud

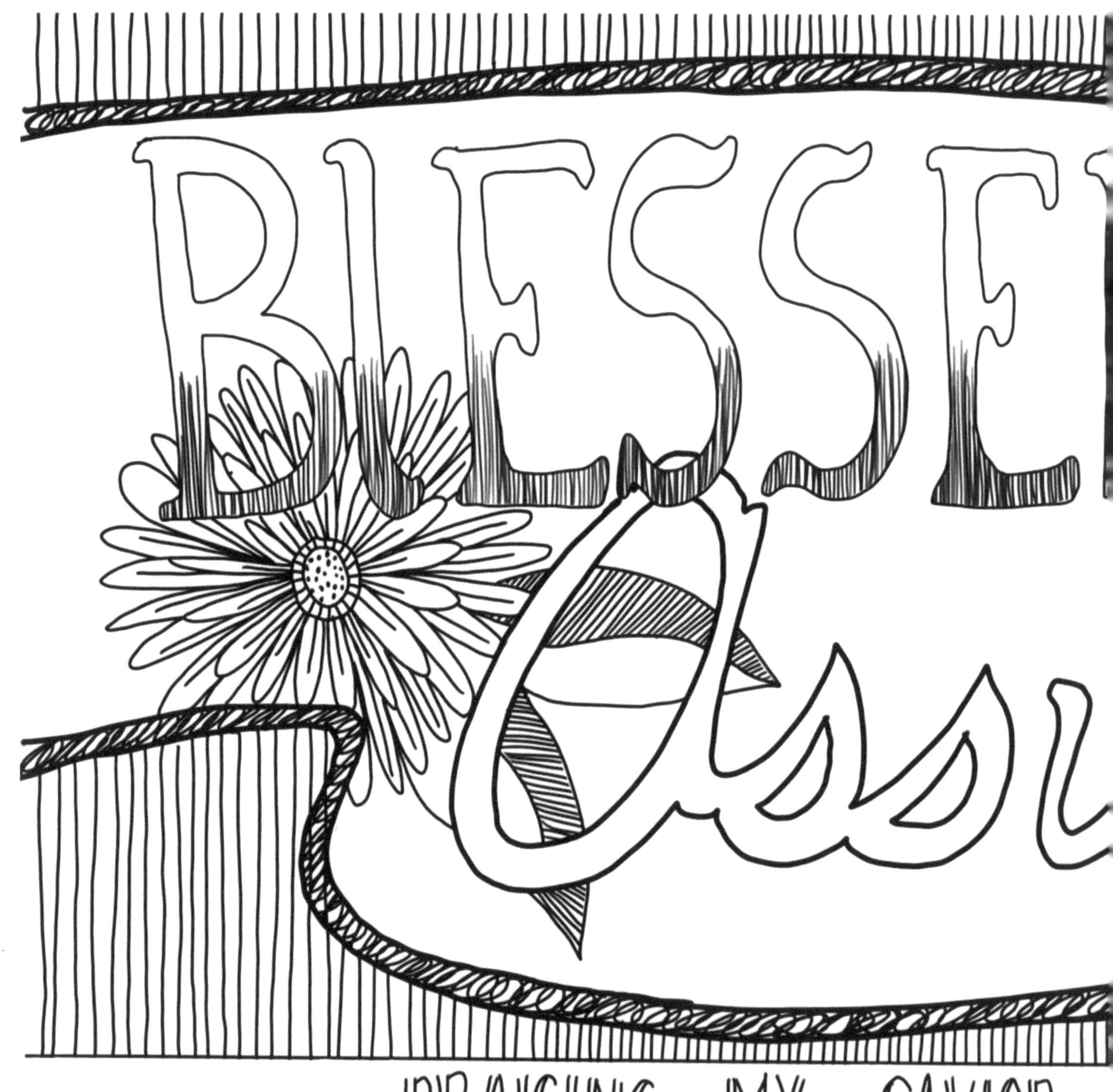

BLESSED
Assu
PRAISING MY SAVIOR

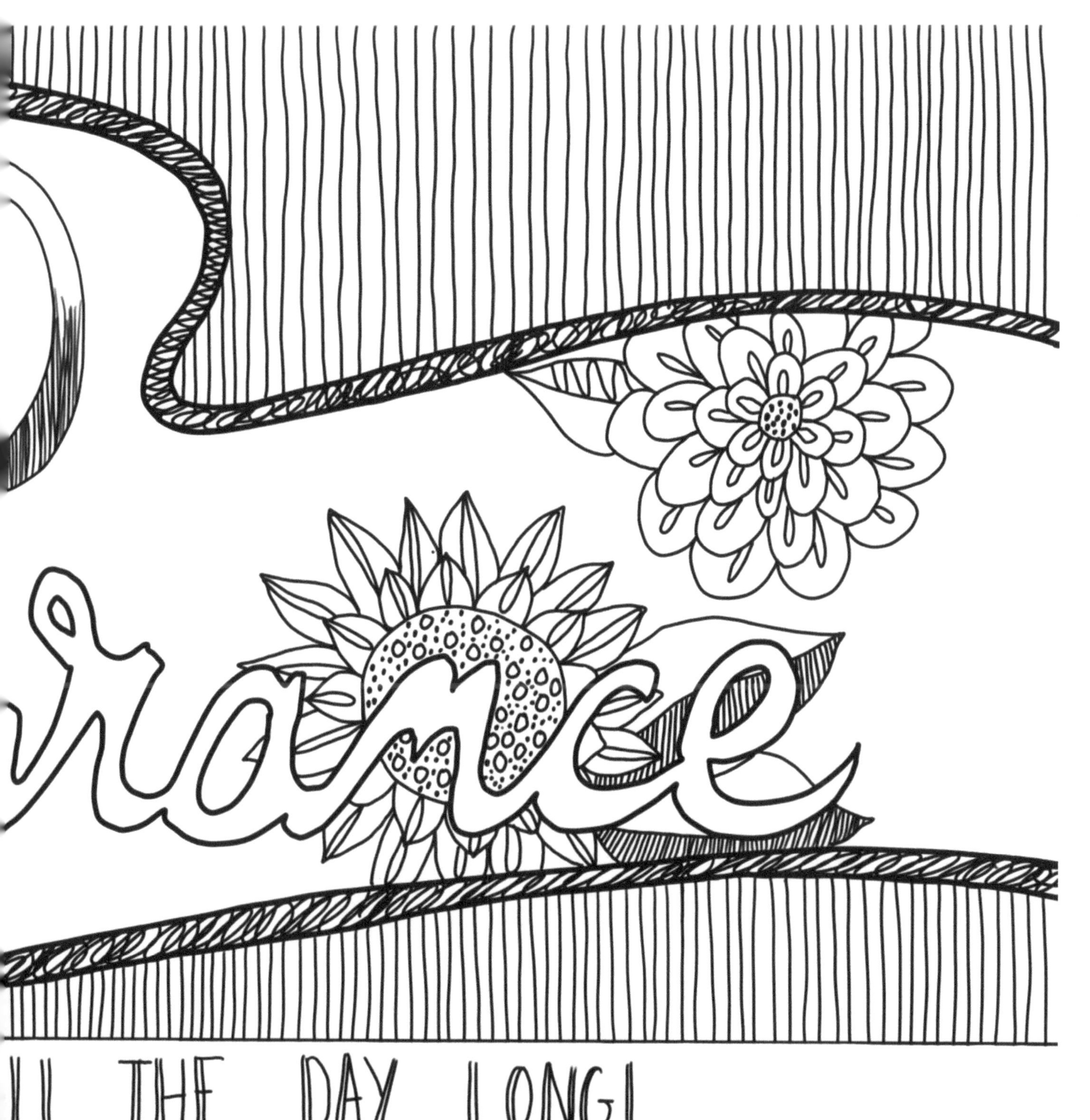

rance
LL THE DAY LONG!

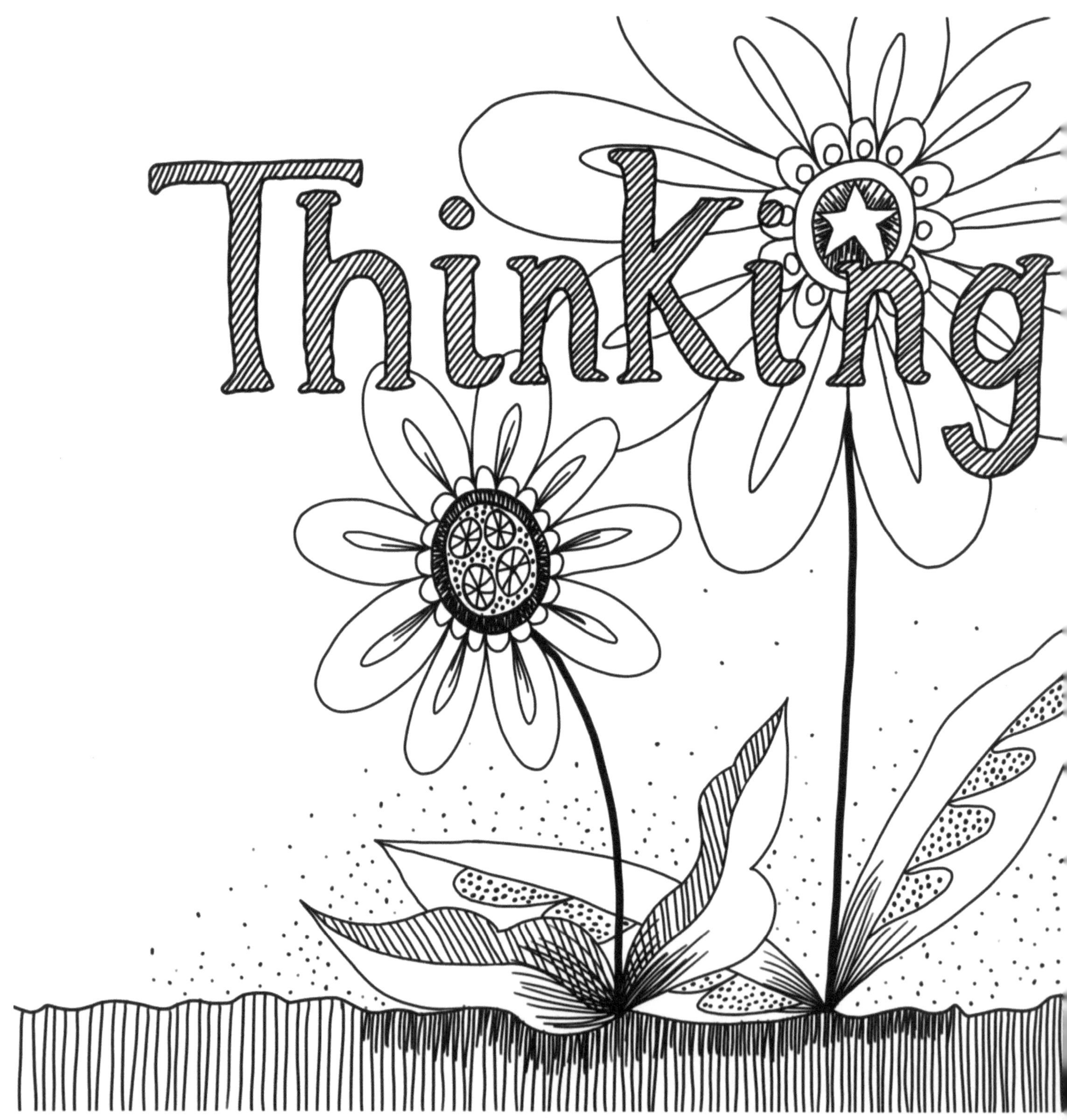
Thinking

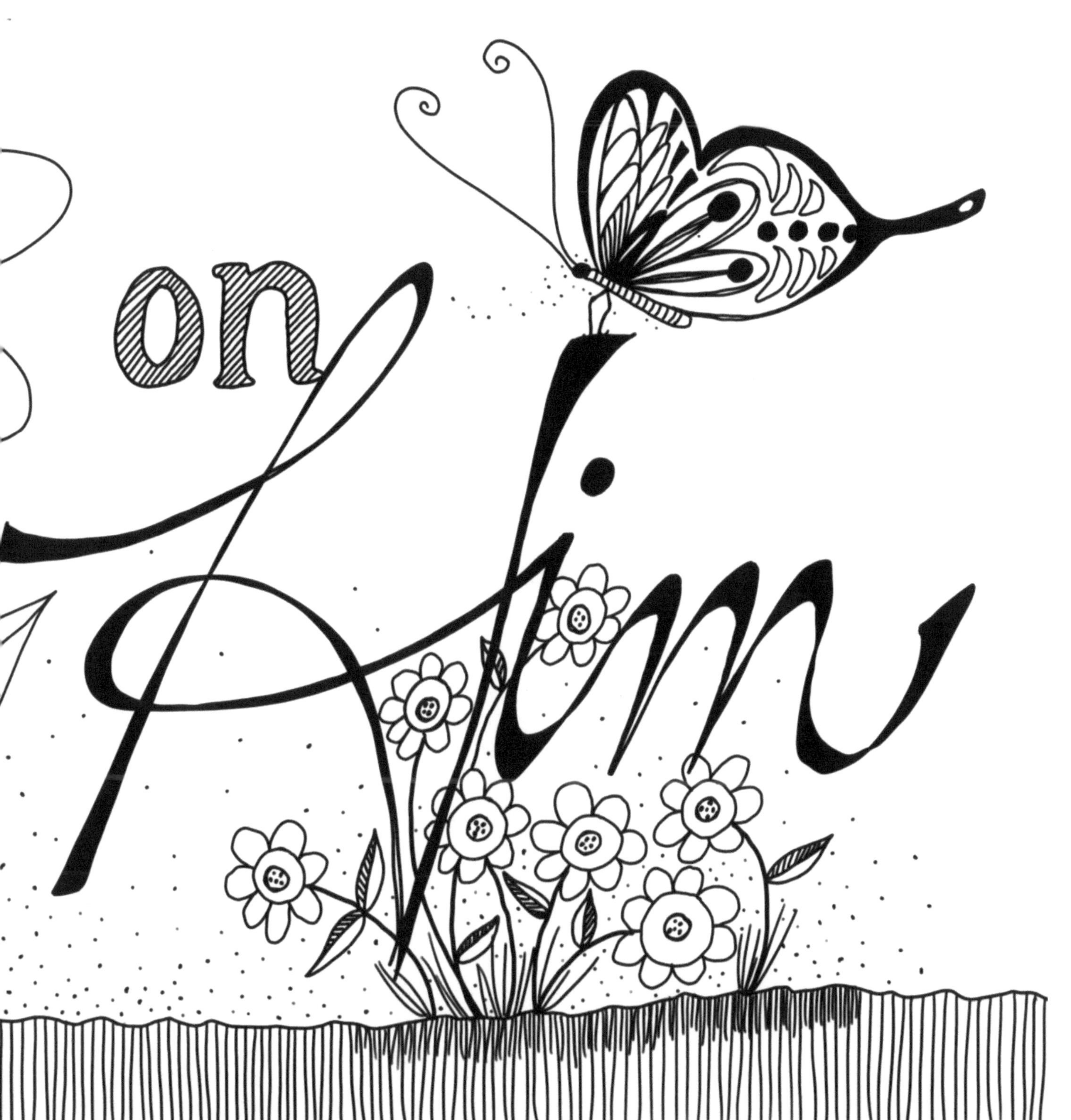
on Him

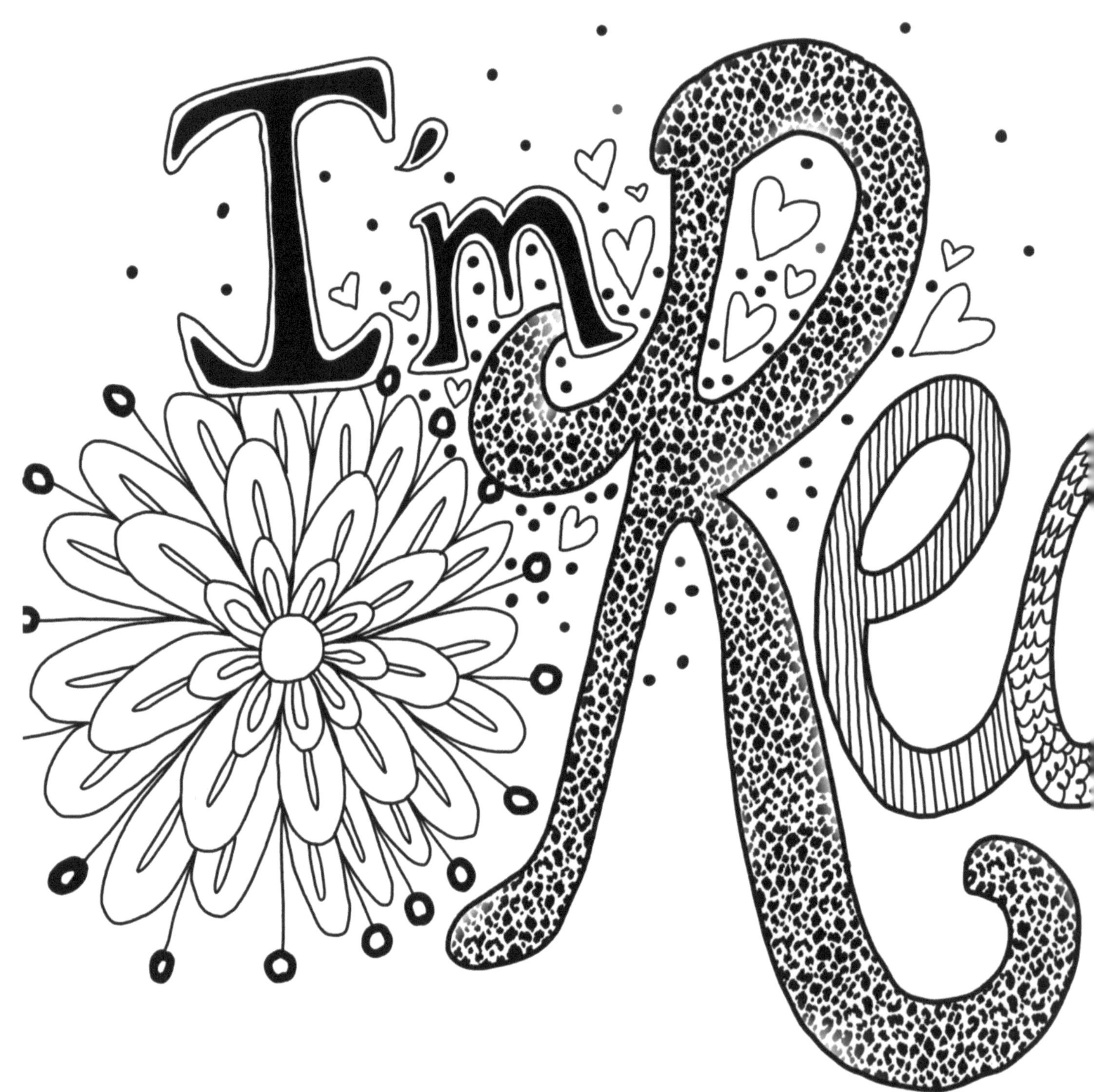

I'm Keg

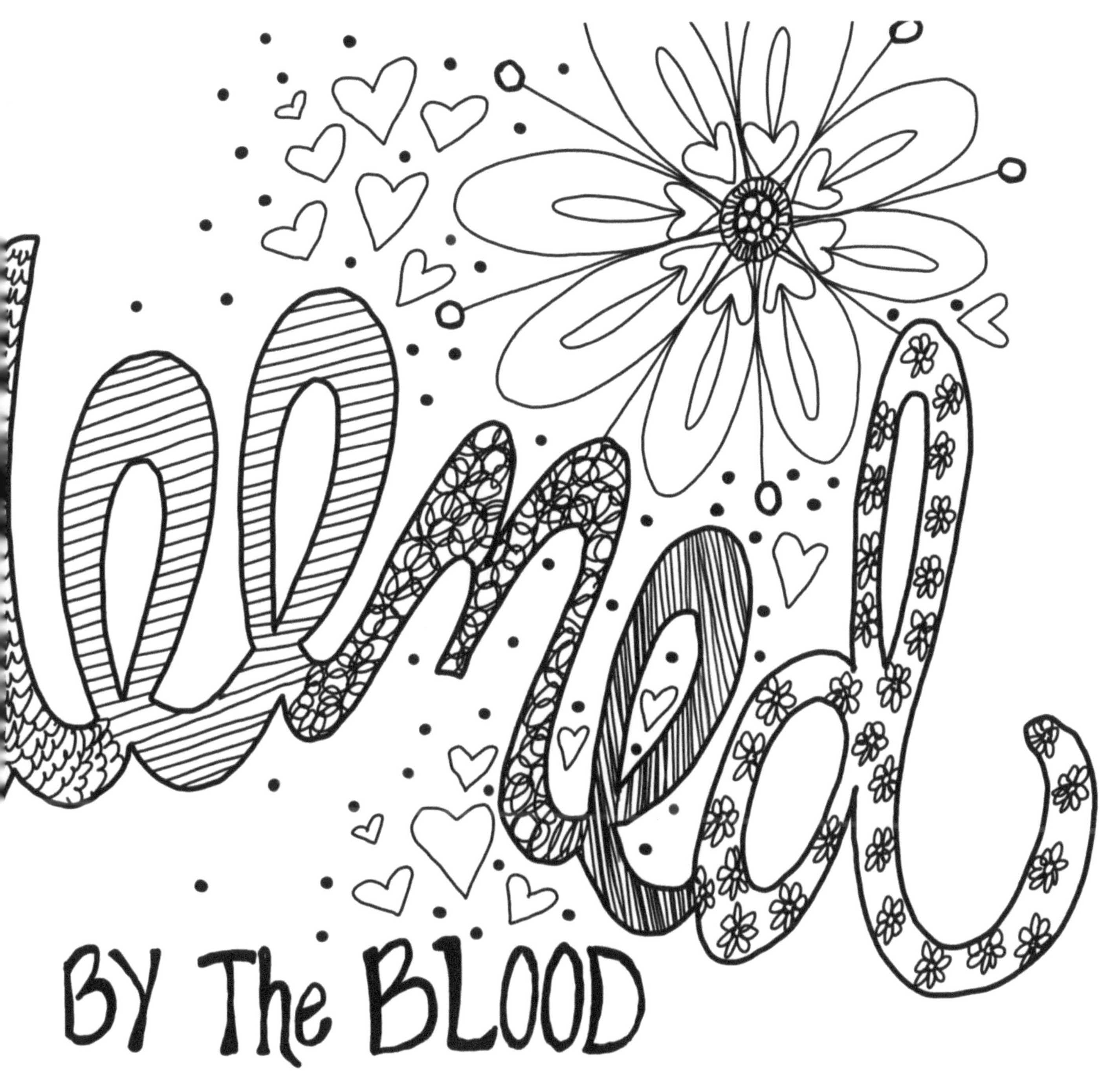

redeemed
BY THE BLOOD

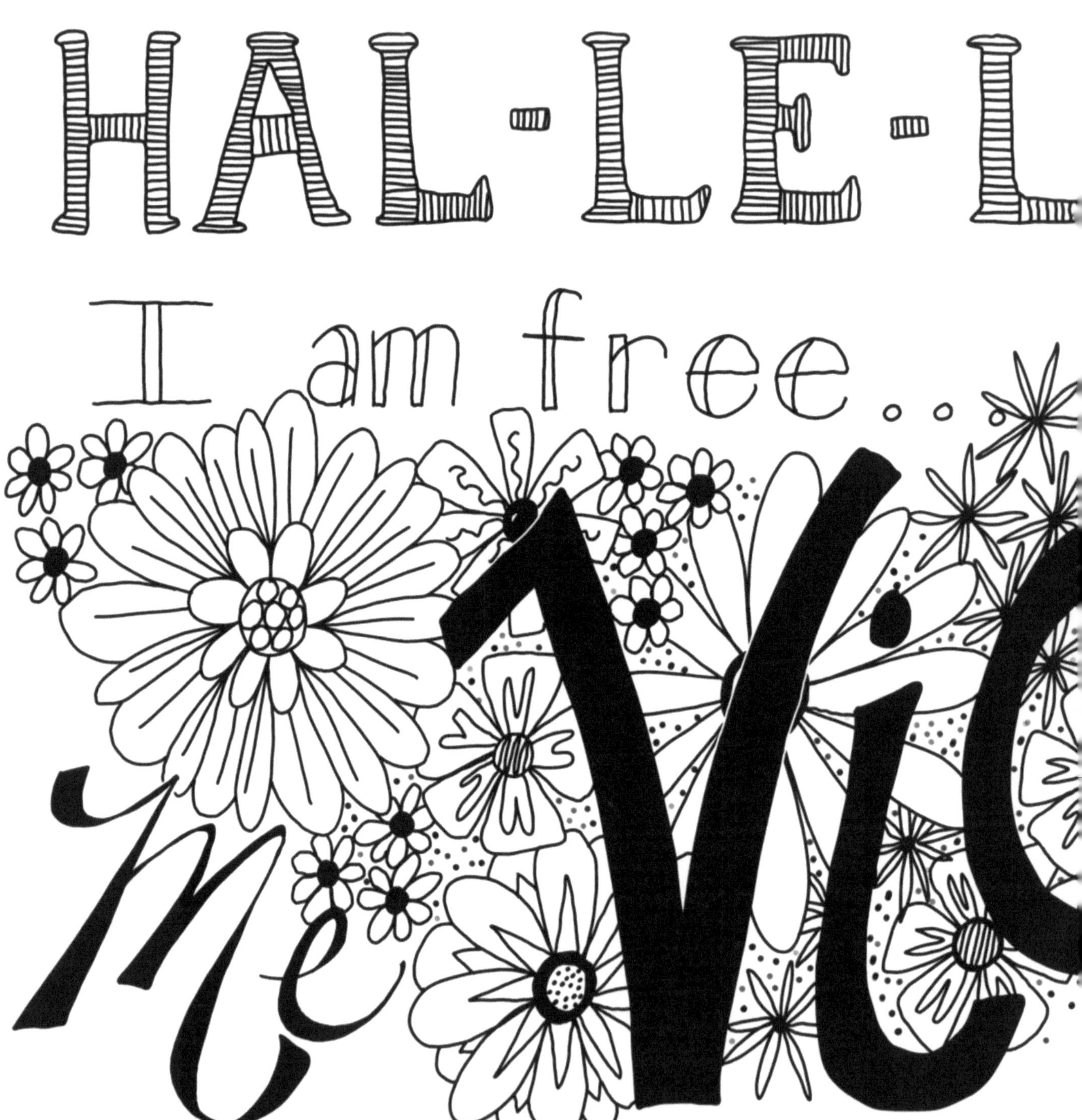

HAL·LE·L
I am free...
Me
Vic

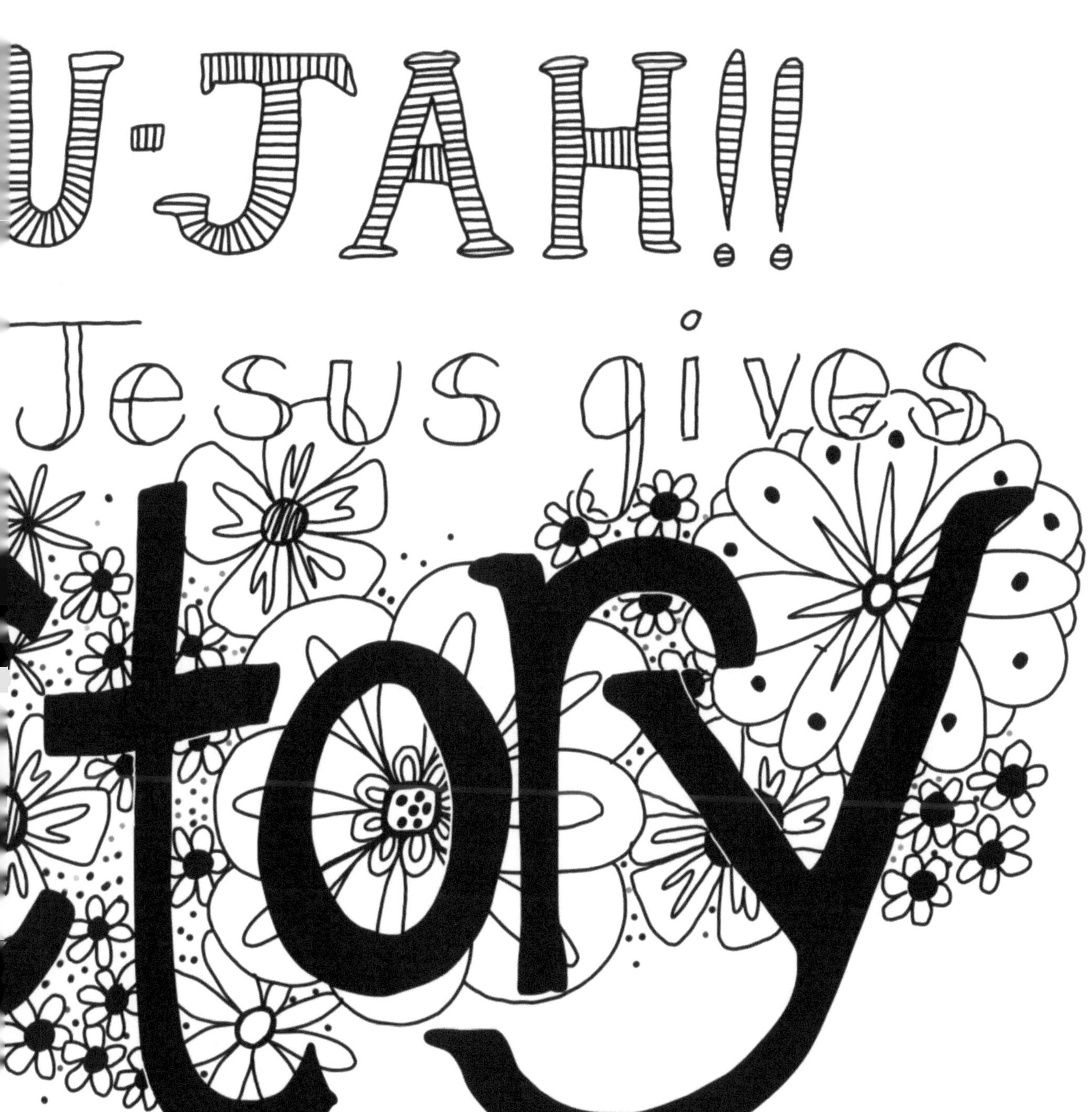
U-JAH!!
Jesus gives
story

A girl and her God.
I was raised in church. At the age of 14, I decided that I wanted to live for God. I don't
remember going to an alter at church. In a quiet moment at home I asked God for forgiveness
and I set my mind that this was the course for me. I was going to live for God. I felt as deeply
committed as a 14 year old girl can about it. After my internal decision I remember being with
my dad in the car, just he and I, and telling him I was going to live for God. I don't remember
him being very dramatic about it. I think he said something along the lines of that was the
best way to approach life. And then we moved on, sitting quietly in the car as he drove.  Later
that summer our church had a meeting and I asked to be baptized…yes, in a creek.

But let's talk about that choice to live for God.  I have never wavered on my decision. But,
there have been many ups and downs.  Let's be clear…God didn't have ups and downs I did.
In my immature young self I would get distracted and caught up in life.  I would be less
attentive to listening to God.  Don't worry, he always gently, or sometimes firmly got my
attention and guided me back to the path I had chosen.  I am ever so thankful for that.  In my
human inadequacy I have begged him over and over to keep me in the center of his will.  So
when I got distracted he was ever so faithful to show me, and keep me on the path.

Through raising my daughter, work life and early marriage my daily devotion with God was
grab and go.  Get a moment, read a verse. I throughly practiced the pray with out ceasing, as
it felt like I never had long moments of time to devote to sitting and meditating on things of
God.  But then as life does, it settled a bit.  I started my morning prayer journal.  I got in a
phase of life where I was able to make time each morning to draw and write.  I spent time in
prayer while I drew in my prayer journal.  It has been such a comfort in my life.  I have all these
beautiful designs and sketches that remind me of answered prayers, heartfelt prayers,
heartache and joy.

I have put this devotional together in hopes that when you have a few minutes of time to
color, think, and pray, you can create beautiful moments of quiet to rest your heart and soul.


Sincerely,
Janita

Marita

FINE ARTIST

Marita is a fine artist and illustrator that lives in south Louisiana. She enjoys her family, gardening, and pets. You can follow her on her creative journey at her website **www.maritagentry.com.** You can join her newsletter and follow her different social media links.